How to Create Your Own Painted Lady

IRVIN ASSOCIATES
Architects   Builders

22½ North Main
Fort Scott, KS 66701
316-223-2564

Ⓐ

Ⓒ

Ⓒ (dots)

Ⓑ (SQUARES)
Ⓔ (BACKGROUND)

Ⓐ
Ⓒ
Ⓔ
Ⓑ
Ⓒ
Ⓒ
Ⓑ

Ⓒ (EDGES)

Ⓑ

Ⓐ

Ⓕ
Ⓓ
Ⓒ

Ⓒ

Ⓐ

Ⓐ

Ⓕ

Ⓔ

Ⓓ

Ⓔ

Ⓑ Ⓒ

Ⓒ Ⓑ Ⓔ

Ⓐ

Ⓕ

Ⓒ (BACKGROUND)
Ⓔ (FOREGROUND)

R SPOKAWSK?

Ⓔ (BLOCK)
Ⓒ (dots)

Elizabeth Pomada
and
Michael Larsen

HOW TO CREATE YOUR OWN PAINTED LADY

A Comprehensive Guide to Beautifying Your Victorian Home

Line Drawings by
Richard Spokowski

Color Renderings by
Carole Glosenger Design

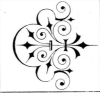

E. P. Dutton
NEW YORK

This book is dedicated to
the homeowners it inspires
to enrich the palette
of America's Victorian rainbow

(*Frontispiece*)

David Irvin's rendering for The Embellished Queen Anne.

Unless otherwise noted, the photographs in this book are by Douglas Keister (DK) or Robert Dufort of Magic Brush (RD).

Contents

Acknowledgments

How to Create a Painted Lady is the most collaborative book we've ever done. Its virtues are the result of the kindness of many people. We are delighted to have this chance to thank the people who contributed their time and creativity to make this book possible.

First thanks go to our editor, Cyril I. Nelson, for suggesting the idea for the book, and then for his help, encouragement, good taste, and dedication in making the book as good as it is.

Thanks also to:

• The six colorists—Doni Tunheim, Jill Pilaroscia, James Martin, David Irvin, Bob Buckter, and Joe Adamo—for their generosity in creating the designs that make this book a work of art, in sharing their wisdom about how they work their magic, and for their portraits.

• James Martin for permission to use his questionnaire.

• Robert Dufort for the story and photographs of his transformation of 1198 Fulton and his own home.

• Carole Glosenger for her beautiful renderings and her perseverance in overcoming unexpected obstacles in drawing them.

• Roger Moss for contributing his insight into how these homes were originally painted, and for his permission to use the Pictorial Glossary.

• Doug Keister for his fine photographs.

• Gustavo Caldavelli of Cal Crew for sharing his knowledge about paint and painting, his help with the photos of materials, and the use of the sample contract.

• Dick Weiss and Lynne Marsden, then at the National Paint & Coatings Association, for their encouragement and for providing the color wheel. Although the NPCA cannot endorse specific products, Judy Hittman and the staff did read the manuscript for technical accuracy.

• Wyman Chin of Creative Paint & Wallpaper in San Francisco for sharing his expertise on paint.

Thanks to Tonia Anderson, Denny Nolan, Wyman Chin, Christy Cizek, Clark Chelsey, and Bruce Nelson for going over the manuscript and offering their sound advice.

For their continuing encouragement and support, we'd like to thank Rita Pomada and Ray and Maryann Larsen.

A Primer on Paint

"To paint your own house is a tale of foolishness, brute force, ignorance, stupidity, and terror—and ultimate joy."

This disgruntled homeowner was in agony while in the throes of doing it himself. But once the job was done, and the blisters from using paint brushes stopped hurting, he was pleased as punch that he finished the job by himself and wouldn't have done it any other way.

This is the fix-it generation. Victorian homeowners all over the country are proudly turning their depressing gray elephants into glorious Painted Ladies. The transformation takes time, love, and money, and the best way to save money is to do it yourself.

American homeowners are embracing a new romanticism reminiscent of the enthusiasm exhibited by homemakers of the last century. They desire, to quote a writer of the Victorian era: "To make home what it should be—a cheerful, happy habitation, to which the absent members of a family may look with love, and to which the wanderer will always return with joy."

In 1883, George Pelz wrote enthusiastically: "Never before was there so general an interest in the decoration of homes as there is today. A truer conception of what home should be is everywhere prevailing. It is not a mere barracks, where a family may congregate and sleep and eat, but it is a place of enjoyment and repose....Nothing which offends can be tolerated there. Beauty—which in the old Roman tongue was *decor*—is home's presiding genius. To *decor*ate home is to bring it under beauty's sway."

Why are homeowners restoring Victorians rather than ripping them down? Because the old houses are made with materials and workmanship that are not reproducible today. There's also the pride and satisfaction in preserving part of our cultural heritage for future generations.

Tasks such as wiring and plumbing usually must be done by licensed professionals because of today's building codes. But you can do the "finish work" on your home—the painting, papering, and plastering that is so labor intensive.

Painted Ladies, once a term for the world's oldest profession, now means:
• a Victorian building, built during Queen Victoria's reign, 1837–1901
• a structure painted in three or more contrasting colors in a balanced, felicitous blend of color and architecture
• a style in which the color is used to bring out the decorative ruffles and flourishes

What was innovative two decades ago at the beginning of The Colorist Movement in San Francisco is now a new tradition. Victorian homeowners are restoring with whimsy and playfulness.

How to Create Your Own Painted Lady will show you how six of the top color designers in America would paint six typical Victorians. This will show you how different the same house can look when you change the palette and give you ideas about painting your own home.

At the back of the book you'll also find black-and-white drawings of each of the six Victorians. Photocopy them, enlarge them if you wish, and try out your own color schemes before working on your house.

To help show you how to beautify your own Painted Lady, the book includes an illustrated step-by-step job by Magic Brush of San Francisco.

But before the work comes "the homework"—in which we'll explain what paint is, how to choose it, what color is, and how to choose and place it. Then we'll offer tips on how to paint and what materials to use. The more you know before starting, the less you'll feel like that disgruntled Do-It-Yourselfer.

What Is Paint?

The Old-House Journal defines *paint* as a barrier, a sacrificial, renewable film that protects a house. Paint is also a cosmetic, a means to bring out the best in the architecture of a building. As any beautician will tell you, the application of cosmetics is a subtle skill. The trick is to enhance the best features with taste. Since you have to paint your house regularly to protect it, you may as well do it creatively.

Paint is coloring pigments mixed with liquid, held together by a binder. Dry pigment provides color, while the liquid carries and holds the pigment to the surface. The binder in oil-based paints was usually linseed oil. Oil-based paints are now usually alkyd-resin–based. The binder in water-based paints is latex resin or, the paint of choice today, vinyl acrylic. Oil-based paints are thinned with organic solvents such as mineral spirits or turpentine, while water-based paints are thinned with water.

The binder is the most expensive part of paint, so cheap paint usually means a shorter life for the paint. Pigment used to be white lead carbonate, which was outlawed in the 1970s for almost all consumer paints. Pigment is either prime or extender. Prime is titanium dioxide, which is white. It has a strong "hiding" ability, meaning that one coat will usually cover, or hide, what's underneath.

Since 85 percent of all tints are white- or light-based, most of these paints start with titanium dioxide. An extender in paint, such as calcium carbonate or aluminum silicate, is simply a filler, which lessens the paint's quality in direct proportion to the amount added. An extender extends the paint, makes it cover more space, but lessens the paint's hiding ability. When zinc oxide is added in paint, it aids color retention and helps fight mildew. By the way, paints called "painter's brands" are not good buys—they're cheaper because they use inferior ingredients.

Paint's Past

Until the nineteenth century, colors were mixed on-site by the painter. Oil paint was usually linseed oil–based, perhaps with white lead as a color base. Michelangelo used raw linseed oil-based paint. Water-based paint was cheap, sometimes just slaked lime and water with glue or crushed oyster shells. Milk and chalky calcimine were also used as water-soluble bases.

Colored with blood, milk paint was exceptionally long-lasting. What we think of as Colonial gray was just blueberries mixed in milk. The color red came from clay or from trees such as brazilwood. Carmine came from dried insect bodies. Blue was from cobalt ore. The rare, expensive, Prussian blue came from prussic acid; ultramarine from lapis lazuli. Copper ore produced green; acetic acid yielded verdigris. Burnt sienna came from iron and manganese. Saffron filaments and buckthorn berries produced two shades of yellow. Three more came from sulfur, mercury, and arsenic. Burnt peach pits made a deep blue-black. Wine lees made Frankfurt black.

Architects of 100 years ago could choose some colors that are no longer available. The color spectrum has not changed. All of the shadings being used now were available then. But some colors used then are not available now because of the concern for safety and ecology.

To see how relatively easy it can be to make paint, look at the formula devised by nineteenth-century architect A. J. Downing: "The colors are supposed to be first finely ground in oil, and then mixed in small quantities with white lead and boiled linseed oil. A few trials will enable the novice to mix agreeable neutral shades—especially if he will be content to add a very little of the darker shades at a time and try the effect with the brush. After the proper shade is obtained, enough should be mixed at once to go over the whole surface."

How to Choose Paint

Of all the improvements one can make on a building, paint is the most reversible. The paint you choose will depend on your budget and the purpose of the paint.

The price per gallon is a factor, but remember that cost efficiency is important too. Saving money today may mean having to spend more sooner than you would have had you used a top-quality paint.

Choosing paint is becoming more difficult as laws and formulas change. In California, for instance, lead was banned in 1976, and certain toxic chemicals that pollute the atmosphere as the paint dries cannot be used. Until recently, most painters chose oil-based paints for old wooden structures because they had originally been painted with oil-based paints. Some oil-based paints had more intense colors and lasted longer. The new formulas that comply with the new laws have not been proven. No one knows how they'll hold up. Acrylics have gotten better at retaining their color and sheen.

Do you want an oil/alkyd-based paint or an acrylic? Oil is traditional. Latex is easier because it cleans with water and can be put on when the weather is damp, unlike oil. Latex is better on new surfaces than oil/alkyd paint.

Latex is best for color and gloss retention. It dries faster. Its finish makes touch-ups easier. Oil or alkyd paint is better for stain resistance and sometimes helps control chalking, which makes the paint self-cleaning when the rain washes the chalk off with the dirt. Oils are glossier than latexes and have greater hiding and penetrating power.

Latex paints are easier to apply than oil/alkyd-based paints. But brush strokes are more visible with water-based than with oil-based paint, and when brush strokes are visible the paints don't level well. This means that the underlying surface shows through and necessitates a second coat.

Latex paint dries in a few hours. Oil/alkyd paint takes at least twenty-four hours. Cleaning up is easier with latex paints. All you need is soap and water. For alkyd paints, you'll need turpentine and paint thinner, which are difficult to dispose of legally.

Once you've chosen between latex and oil/alkyd, you'll need to choose brands. When choosing the different paints, whether factory-mixed or custom-mixed to your specifications, choose either the same brand or brands that work well together.

Hiding is crucial. The fewer coats you need, the easier and cheaper the job. Fewer coats also mean less risk of peeling and cracking on built-up layers.

Which paint you choose also depends on the colors you choose. Some pigments cost more money. Yellows and bright colors are the most expensive because you usually need two coats. Gray can be very inexpensive.

Some colors last longer than others. Colors can fade in sunlight. Light yellows, for example are susceptible to fading from ultraviolet rays. In the South, greens fade to light blue. Oil-based red can turn into an unattractive pink. White doesn't fade, but it can yellow in the shade, especially if there's linseed oil in the paint.

Erosion is a factor with some brands. Erosion can clean your house, especially with white paint, since the paint sloughs off and takes dirt and light mildew with it. Sunlight kills mildew, which can be a problem on the shady north side of a house. Latex usually resists mildew better than oil/alkyd-based paint.

Darker colors resist dirt better than lighter colors, but this is true only with a durable paint. Some deep blues can fade in two or three months. However, factory-ground colors make a dark paint longer-lasting. Both the Fuller O'Brien and Benjamin Moore paint brands have deep, dark, factory-ground colors. The deepest, darkest, most intense colors work best when based on dark, pure, factory-ground colors.

Many companies have only a white- or clear-base system, which means that the base of the paint is white. The white system starts with five basically white bases: bone white, pastel, medium, deep, and ultra-deep white. The lightest one can only accept a minimum amount of pigment. If you inject more color or pigment than the paint can hold, the color will "float," or rise to the surface, and separate from the paint. So to get a darker shade, you go to the next darker base. But because you're injecting color into white, there's more fading.

If you want a deep or intense color, start with a major paint brand that has a factory-ground base closest to the one you want. Then mix it with standard factory-ground colors. You can combine up to three factory-ground colors for good results.

Coverage—how well the paint will cover the surface when put on the wall—also depends on color. A pastel may need two or three coats to be completely opaque.

Add a small amount of raw umber, raw sienna, or lampblack to help with coverage when using pastel paints. You may also have to compensate with a lighter version of your chosen pastel that, when mixed with the dark additive, will result in the right shade. That little bit of dark base will make the paint look better longer.

Sheens

Finishes range from flat to glossy. The shine of the dried paint determines its patina or sheen. Gloss is the shiniest. Next is semigloss, then eggshell or satin, then flat, which has no shine. A glossy finish makes color appear brighter, deeper, and stronger than a flat finish. Flat sheens make colors recede and glosses make them jump out.

The patina or sheen can change the intensity and value of the color. You can use an intense color with a patina that makes the color look softer and not as bold. For example, flat finishes, which absorb light, are not as intense as semigloss finishes. So a vivid purple will look brighter with a semigloss finish than it will in a flat finish.

A flat finish will minimize surface irregularity. A glossy finish is smoother, easier to clean. Most oil/alkyd paints are glossy, but latex holds its gloss better. High gloss is the most durable.

Various sheens may be used on the same façade, so long as you don't mix oil- and water-based paint together. Variations on sheen add dimension to a paint job. San Francisco colorist Bob Buckter recommends satin on the main body, semigloss on the major trim, and flat on small, well-balanced accent areas. You can use an oil-based trim paint next to a flat latex or satin acrylic.

How Much Is Enough?

Here's how to compute how much paint to buy. The distance around the house—the perimeter—multiplied by the height gives the total area in square feet below the roof line. For each pitched roof or gable, multiply the height of the peak from the roof base by half the length of the base. Add the peak-area square footage to the below-roof-line square footage for the total.

If you plan to use a different paint for the trim, subtract the total area of the doors and window frames. One gallon of paint will cover about 300 to 400 square feet, depending on the nature and condition of the surface it covers, so divide your total square footage by 300 or 400. Buy more for touch-ups. Buy twice the amount if you need two coats.

The Smiles of Nature

"Colors are the smiles of nature."
—Nineteenth-century English poet Leigh Hunt

"To master colour is to exercise in secret...an almost despotic power over human thoughts and feelings," *The Paper Hanger & Decorator's Assistant* warned a century ago. You don't have to be a color specialist to know that some colors make you happy, others make you sad. To understand colors better, look at the color wheel.

All colors are made from three *primary* colors: red, yellow, and blue. The green, violet, and orange that border these colors on the color wheel, and that are made by mixing two primary colors, are called *secondary* or *complementary* colors. Equal amounts of complementary colors produce gray when combined. *Tertiary* colors are each primary color mixed with those on both sides of it on a color wheel: olive, russet, and citrine. Black and white are *neutral* colors.

The intensity or saturation of a color, or *hue*, is called *chroma*. *Intensity* is the brilliance or saturation, the mildness or denseness, of a color. Primaries are high chroma, and grayed colors have low chroma. A *tint* is a hue lightened by white. *Shades* are colors or hues that are grayed—that is, darkened—with black. *Value* is the light-to-dark scale, the lightness or darkness of a color.

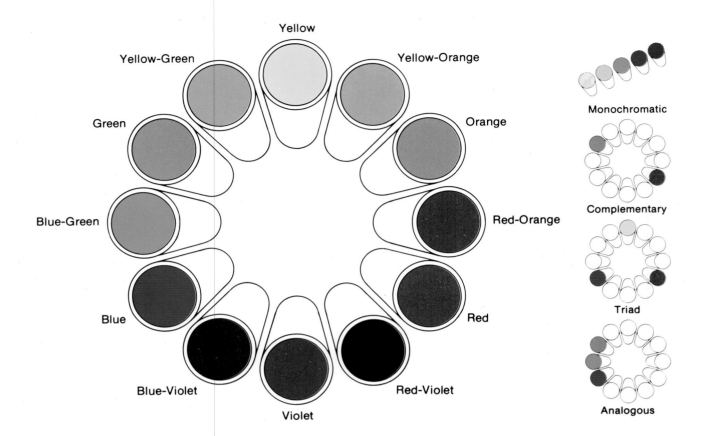

Blue is cold, orange is warm or fiery, yellow is bright and advancing. Violet is receding, red is hot and glaring. Green is quiet and cool. Colors that recede are pale, cool colors. Colors that advance are dark, bright, warm colors.

There are four kinds of color schemes:

Monochromatic: all one color

Complementary: colors opposite each other on color wheel

Triad: three colors that are equidistant on the color wheel

Analogous: three colors next to each other on the color wheel—green, blue-green, and blue, for example. But you would use more of one color than the others in an analogous palette.

When choosing colors, choose a color palette in which there is a relationship of both hue and value running through all the colors. In practical terms, this may mean mixing in a little of each color with the one next to it when painting highly contrasting colors on a house. This little bit of mixing helps to create harmony between colors.

A Battle on Canvas

In 1876, Isaac H. Hobbs wrote: "Designing a building is like a battle upon canvas of color, each part striving for supremacy." He urged Americans to "study their picturesque use of external colors. And let the walls of our cities assume new life and meaning by contrasting tints of various bricks, stones, and brilliant tiles."

Even Andrew Jackson Downing said that the exterior color of a house "is of more importance than is usually supposed, since, next to the form itself, the color is the first impression which the eye receives in approaching it.

"Its features confer a kind of expression on a house that the eyes, eyebrows, lips, etc., of a face do upon the human countenance....A certain sprightliness is therefore always bestowed on a dwelling in a neutral tint, by painting the bolder projecting features a different shade."

In the 1880s the Devoe Paint Company advised that: "The many fronts, diversified as to material, with visible framing, shingle or smooth covering, the gables, the porches, etc., all provide a means for the employment of particolored effects, the most attractive and artistically valuable feature of modern house painting."

Before you choose colors for your Painted Lady, you'll have to decide whether to use a historical or contemporary color scheme. Many paint companies offer palettes called *traditional* or *historical*, but they publish the palettes to promote their paint, and some of the colors deemed authentic are not necessarily so. Chemical formulas have changed over the years as have tastes.

You may prefer strong colors to quiet ones. You may also want to identify and reproduce the colors that were on your house when it was built, but this is not as easy as it sounds. To determine original colors, cut through all the paint layers, then sand the bottom, or first layer with a fine sandpaper, lubricate it with colorless oil, and then examine it with a magnifying glass.

However, the yellow ochre or Spanish brown you will be looking at will probably be a combination of primer, time, and degenerating paint, not a true finish coat. Paint frequently degenerates to a yellowish or greenish tan. Verdigris turns black. Consider mailing samples to a specialist for a microanalysis of paint chips, both chemical and spectrographic examinations, which can cost $50 and up per sample. Take two samples from each area where there may be different paint colors, such as the body, the accent, and the trim.

You can learn even more about authentic color schemes by reading Roger W. Moss and Gail Caskey Winkler's *Victorian Exterior Decoration* and *Daughters of Painted Ladies*.

Late Victorian colors often made a strong statement. But it was *their* color statement. Today, you can make your own.

Picture It Pretty

Getting dressed in the morning is a design decision. Paint is a design decision too. Pick out your favorite colors by looking at your clothes and your rooms.

Every house should show its best face. Applying paint is like applying makeup. Paint can create a cosmetic face with lights that minimize flaws and play up a house's best features.

You'll need to choose a base color to use on the siding or walls, one or more trim colors, and an accent color that adds punch to the scheme and makes everything come alive. Once you've chosen the dominant color, add others in varying amounts to give the scheme rhythm.

Color designers suggest using at least four colors, but not more than four if you're unsure of yourself. A two-color scheme may lack dimension and fight the complexity of the building. A three-color scheme is hard to arrange consistently. Four or five colors are needed to enhance an elaborate Victorian's architectural ornamentation. You will discover that you can orchestrate the surface of your house with carefully chosen colors. A conservative philosophy is that the house should enjoy its colors. A contemporary colorist would say that your house should sing.

Different regions of the country prefer different colors. Keep in mind the street where you live. Your house has to live there, too. See how your house looks in comparison to its neighbors.

Look at your house from the street, across the street, and up close. Decide what features you like or don't like.

What are the givens? What direction does it face? Is it shaded or in full sun? The light it gets will affect its colors. The shade from surrounding trees can also change the house's colors with the seasons.

A shaded house that faces south or west could be glaringly bright and may need cool colors. A house under huge oak trees will appear dead if painted with too somber a shade. Consider gray-green trimmed with white to give the impression of highlights made by the sun. You can make it sparkle with magenta accents.

Take a black-and-white photograph of the house and enlarge it to 8 by 10 inches. Then trace the picture onto plain white paper. The tracing gets you in touch with the house. You may even find details you weren't aware of. Make copies of the tracing.

Some color designers recommend shooting an entire roll of film of the façade so that you can study details and corners from all angles.

Pay attention to details: the roof—its shape, texture, and color; the chimney mass and material. What are the permanent colors of the house? A red tile roof has to blend with the rest of the house, as does a brick chimney or a gray slate walkway.

What's symmetrical or asymmetrical? Identify and number the elements.

You'll have to choose color for the trim around the roof, the vertical lines, the trim around the windows, the body of the house.

Do you want to accent the front door? The shutters? Porch railings and other decorative details? The eaves and moldings?

The windows are holes in your canvas, as are the doors. Most, but not all, Victorians considered the windows of a house to be its eyes—to be closed with black or dark sashes. Contemporary Americans prefer the lightness and openness of light-colored sashes.

Your front door opens a dialogue between the outside and inside of your house. The color of the front door suggests what kind of people live inside. A dark-brown front door doesn't look very friendly unless it's polished, gleaming wood. A red door shouts "Welcome!"

What's the architectural style? Do you want to make details, such as gables or gingerbread trim, stand out? Or give height to a small house with a bold color to accent its vertical lines?

Even the colors of your curtains should be taken into consideration.

Work out a personal paint-by-number sheet and try various color combinations. Since a colored pencil sketch can only hint at the more than 1,600 colors available at the paint store, it's better just to use shades

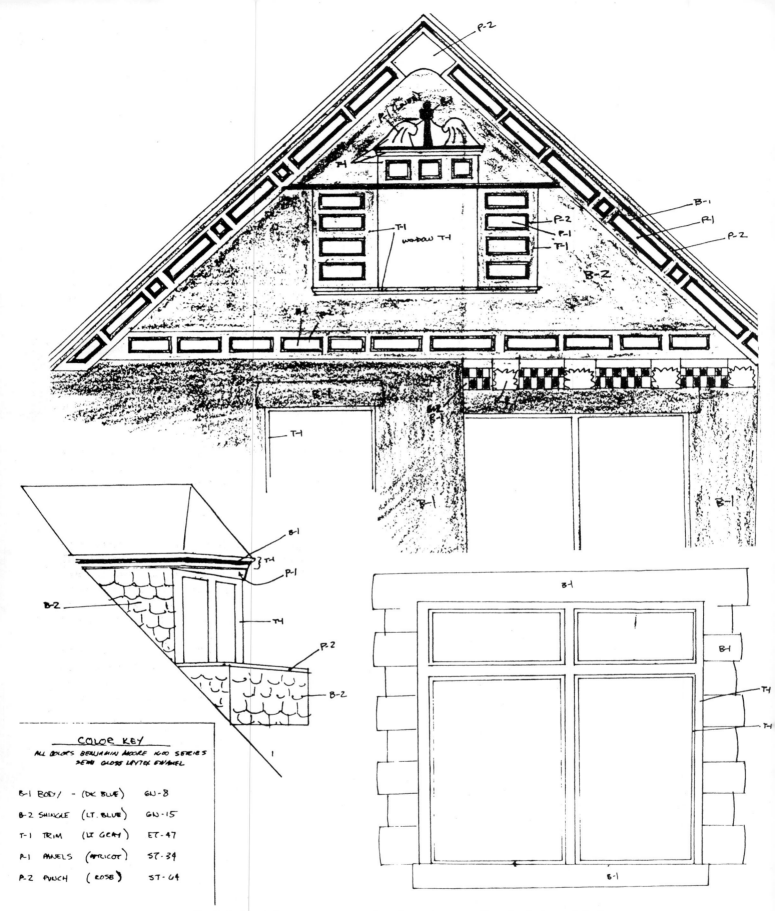

COLOR KEY

ALL COLORS BENJAMIN MOORE 1600 SERIES
SEMI GLOSS LATEX ENAMEL

B-1 BODY / - (DK BLUE)   GN-8

B-2 SHINGLE (LT. BLUE)   GN-15

T-1 TRIM (LT GRAY)   ET-47

P-1 PANELS (APRICOT)   ST-34

P-2 PUNCH (ROSE)   ST-64

Shaded sketch by James Martin that shows how to allow for light and dark values when creating a color scheme.

of dark to light. Look at the pencil sketch James Martin has provided to get an idea of what such a shaded sketch will look like.

When you've made an initial choice, take your paint samples outside and look at them in natural light, for color is, of course, an interaction of light. Look at paint chips on a white background and make sure that they touch each other when you're mixing and matching. A yellow swatch will look different in front of a navy coat and a white shirt. Paint store computers can come close to matching any color you choose.

When you've found the body color or colors you like, try different trim colors until one works. Make sure these colors correspond in value—lightness and darkness—to the tracing you've made.

Light colors shadow more than dark ones and can show imperfections. Use dark colors to play down problem areas. Light projects, so use light colors on projecting elements. Dark recedes, so use dark colors on receding elements. Use dark at the bottom; light at the top.

Change color whenever the plane of the building changes. These color changes, or breaks between colors, will enhance and highlight the architectural components.

Bright color is usually best when it is used on a small area. Color intensity is greater on a large scale. Ultraviolet may be vibrant as an accent, but it would be overpowering as a major trim color. Avoid violent contrasts and use transition colors to buffer high-contrast areas.

Buy quarts of your chosen paint and color-test on the house. Check the colors and how they harmonize at dawn, midday, and dusk for several days.

Laying the Foundation

Before you apply the paint and polish on your Painted Lady, make sure the house is in order. If you are restoring, you'll have to decide whether you want an authentic restoration or an interpretive one. Do some research. See what secrets the house holds by checking in the library or the newspaper morgue. Documents written at the time the house was built are more trustworthy than a neighbor's memory. Even old black-and-white photographs will show that light and dark colors were used at the turn of the century. Few Victorians were all white.

A plan will help throughout the process. Don't do anything drastic or irreversible until you've lived with the house a bit. Let it talk to you.

One homeowner we heard about had to stop listening. His house told him what to paint it, but when he got finished, it told him to buy the house next door.

Remove crumbling wood, plaster, and paint. Finish the roof first, then the interior, starting with plumbing, wiring, and insulation, then the exterior. (However, it may be better to finish windows on the outside before you do them on the inside.) Do all the demolition at the same time. Be sure to remember Murphy's Law of Restoration: It will take twice as long and cost twice as much as originally planned.

Set priorities for yourself. High on the list of priorities should be enduring the turmoil. How will you and your family survive the coming months? Think about the health and psychological aspects of the renovation process.

Get all permits beforehand and hire professionals on all structural work.

Save historic elements such as glass, panels, and ornamental plaster by storing them safely while havoc reigns. Shield good wooden floors and unpainted woodwork. Clean up before you throw anything out, so you know what you're throwing out.

Photograph or video every step of the way as a record for yourself and future owners, and for possible use if you decide to list your house on the National Register. Photos may help replace items in their correct location. The video or photographs will also provide "remember when" laughs later. *Victorian Homes* or *The Old-House Journal* might even want a story about your efforts.

As in all things, start with the foundation and work your way up. If you have to raise your home to add a garage, do it before you fix the roof.

Prep School

Preparation is the most important step in restoring a Victorian. This means stripping it down to bare wood, if necessary, sealing it, then starting to paint. Scrape, burn, or chemically strip. Sandblasting is recommended only on stucco. Southern and western exposures will have weathering problems because of strong sunlight, winds, and weather.

Take care of a mildew problem at this stage. Years ago, lead and mercury in paint prevented certain problems such as mildew. Today, buildings sometimes have to be treated twice with bleach before painting begins, and sometimes even that doesn't work.

Most paint problems are caused by the loss of flexibility of the existing paint, moisture, and/or poor adhesion of one layer to another. A paint job is only as good as the surface on which it is applied. Some wood may have to be repaired or replaced. Since wood stretches and contracts during heat and cold or as sunlight and humidity change, paint has to be flexible. When paint loses its flexibility, it fails. This is what causes peeling, cracking, crazing, flaking, and alligatoring. Stripping failed paint, correcting nailhead staining, and fixing flashings around the gutters must be done before you paint.

If your state allows chemical paint stripping, try Diedrich 606 Caustic Multi Layer Paint Remover. It softens and dissolves paint for easy wash removal. For a free demonstration movie, call 800-323-3566. Californians have a problem using chemical strippers, because they cannot allow any of the chemical or stripped paint to flow into the ground—they have to collect it all and dispose of it properly.

After you have cleaned the house, you must prep it and caulk it. Do the siding first, then the main trim, and end with the accents. A good prep job can take four to eight hours for every hour of painting.

Before painting, prime the building. The primer provides a bond between the topcoat and the surface to be painted. It prevents the topcoat from penetrating the surface, so there will be an even gloss. With today's primers, you may even apply latex over alkyd paint, and vice versa.

The First Stroke

You've picked your colors, sheen, and finish. Your tools and materials are ready. The surface is clean, filled, and free of moisture and rough spots.

Your first step is to read the label. Stir the paint and start.

To be sure your paint is uniform, buy it all at once. Have the paint store mix it all, and then re-can it. Then pour a small amount in a vessel you can handle comfortably. Seal the rest with transparent plastic wrap before covering. And stir each time you pour out another portion.

Paint on dry days, after the dew has evaporated, but not in direct sunlight. Latex works better when the temperature is over 50 degrees. Follow the instructions on the paint can.

Paint with the grain of the wood. Finish a complete side, at least to a door or window, before stopping for the day. Don't start a new can of paint in the middle of a large area. If the remaining paint won't finish the area, mix some new paint with the partially filled can before starting the area so as to help blend color and give it a uniform appearance.

Paint only with the tips of the brush, not the sides, and immerse the bristles no farther than one-third of their length into the paint. Remove the excess by tapping on the side of the can, not by scraping over the can edges, which removes too much paint.

When using a roller, paint the outside edges with a brush for a neater job.

Don't stretch a can of paint farther than its label suggests.

If you hire help, work closely with your painters every day. Even though you're an amateur, trust your judgment and your instincts.

When you're finished, clean up completely. Store leftover paint for touch-ups.

Regular maintenance checkups will keep problems small and will keep your Painted Lady smiling.

Special Cases

Porch Ceilings. Starting at the back, the point farthest from the steps or entrance, work across the width, not the length, of the porch. This prevents one lap from drying before the next lap is painted. Paint in slightly overlapping strips about 2 feet wide. Paint the edges first, then work to the center and front. Many people in hot climes paint their porch ceiling sky blue to create a cool feeling. The old theory that light blue paint repels wasps, flies, and spiders has yet to be proved.

For woodwork: use a round, 1-inch brush for horizontal and vertical window sashes; use a tapered 2- to 3-inch brush for the rest of the trim.

Roofs. Replace asphalt shingles that have curled or cupped. If your roof is flat, with roll roofing, check the junction of the roof and parapet wall and the flashing for cracking and leakage. Paint metal roofs.

Paint the roof so it will complement the overall color scheme. If a dark color heats up the house too much, use an attic fan or insulation.

Chimneys and Brick. Brickwork must be kept pointed. Repointing brick means applying new mortar between bricks where the original mortar has eroded. First chisel out and wire-brush eroded mortar to reach solid mortar. Don't stint on this work; the wall might fall down. Use a mortar that only requires adding water. Be sure to wet down the wall first by spraying or sponging to ensure that water in the new mortar won't be drawn out by the existing wall before it can set properly. Tuckpoint, or firm and neaten, the mortar with a trowel or a special tool that is made for the purpose. For neatness, work from the top down. Follow the directions on the package of mortar.

Metalwork. It's better to preserve and repair original iron railings than to replace them. Cast iron was made by pouring hot metal into decorative molds, and it is too hard to be shaped by hammering. New pieces can be made to replace missing elements. If the metalwork is wrought iron, take it to a blacksmith for repairs.

Metals should be primed against rust, then painted. If you can find red-lead primer, use it, for it works best. Cast-iron ornaments should be caulked before priming and painting.

Paint gutters. Check the joints and linings.

Galvanized metal is iron or steel with a zinc coating that is used for coping, gutters, roof decks, some cresting, finials, and pediments. Prep before painting using the paint manufacturer's instructions.

Gingerbread. One way to remodel even a plain boxy house is to do what the Victorians did: add sunbursts and sunflowers, spindles, finials, and pendants—anything from corner and foundation boards to cornices and brackets. Victorian homeowners did this with mad abandon. You may wish to be more judicious. Inasmuch as Downing introduced the Italianate style by adding verandas, porches, and window casings, feel free to follow suit. The first Italianates imitated stone castles, and pink shingles on Queen Annes imitated the clay tiles of England.

Sawn-wood ornaments were frequently made out of leftover wood. Homeowners decided what kind of gingerbread they wanted, and then hired carpenters to do the baking.

Doors. Paint the top panels, then the molding edges. Brush across, then up and down. Use three values on a door. The lights should be on the raised panels and the moldings, the darks should be in the recesses. If you use two colors, use two values of each to enhance the play of light and dark.

Steps. Paint the underside of the step extension first, then the back panel, then the horizontal surface.

Windows. Paint the outside sash, then the crossbars, frame, and bottom panel. Masking the window glass with tape isn't always recommended. Instead, apply paint on the glass in a controlled way. Use a tapered brush to push a small bead of paint onto the glass. This covers the glazing putty, which will act as insulation to keep out water. Paint all around the glass first, then go back and fill in the sash, then the frame. Slight variations won't be seen from the street. This saves you the time of removing masking tape and scraping glass with a razor.

Exterior Stains. The use of alkyd and latex semitransparent and opaque stains is new. The stain acts both as a preservative and as a protection against weathering. Maintenance and prepping for a stain finish are easier than using paint, but the surface has to be new or totally stripped. Apply prestain on a new surface.

Staining is recommended in harsh seacoast climates and on decks and with new wood shingles. It can cover stains and fight mildew. Application of a stain finish is more difficult than paint: Pour the top oils out and stir, then put the oils back and stir. Mix one batch of stain into another to avoid pigment concentration and color differences. Stir often. On hot days, dampen the surface before applying latex stain. Oil stain must be used on a dry surface. Remove the trim and work on it separately.

Tools of the Trade

You can find the following tools in any well-stocked paint store.

Brushes, rollers, and paint sprayers. Use a 4-inch brush for siding, 1- to 2-inch sash brush for trim, a roller and tray for flat surfaces.

Paint pad for shingles
Ladders, falls, or scaffolds
A pail hook to hold the paint can on the ladder.
Paper and plastic masking tape to protect surfaces
Wire brushes and paint scrapers
Putty and a putty knife
Caulk and a caulking gun
Sandpaper to smooth rough areas and roughen glossy ones
Cleaners for brushes and roller
Wipe-up cloths
Polyurethane dropcloths so paint doesn't penetrate through to what you're protecting.

Brushing Up

Good-quality brushes save time, elbow grease, and money. Use natural bristle for oil/alkyd-base paints, varnishes, and lacquers because they leave a smooth finish.

Polyester brushes can be used for latex and oil-base paints. They keep their shape and stiffness, apply paint smoothly and evenly in any weather, and they are easy to clean. Nylon/polyester brushes can be used for all paints. They combine the durability of nylon with the shape retention of polyester.

Bristle brushes, made of hog hairs and called China brushes, are used for nonwater-soluble finishes.

Flagged bristles—"ragged" ends—help load the brush and let paint flow smoothly. A good brush is tapered to provide smooth paint release with a fine painting edge. The brush will be full, with no hollow space in the center of the brush. Long flexible bristles of varied lengths hold more paint, and flagged ends leave fewer brush marks.

Bristle length is important for better loading and smoother application. Cheap brushes are too short.

Use 1- and 2-inch brushes for windows, shutters, and

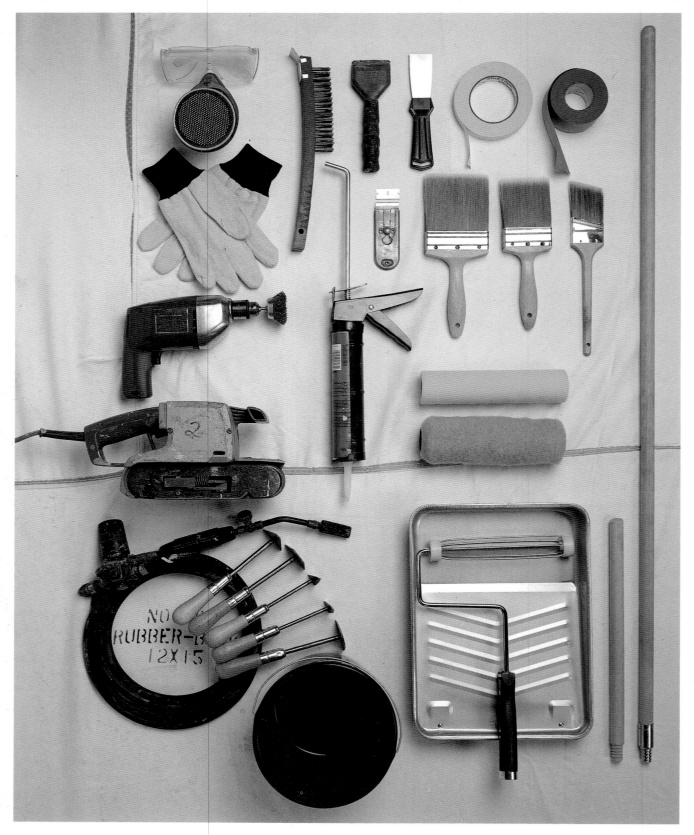

Materials used in painting a house: goggles, mask, gloves, wire brush, scraper, putty knife, masking tapes, brushes and brush extenders, scraper, torches, picks, paint roller, and paint pan. (DK)

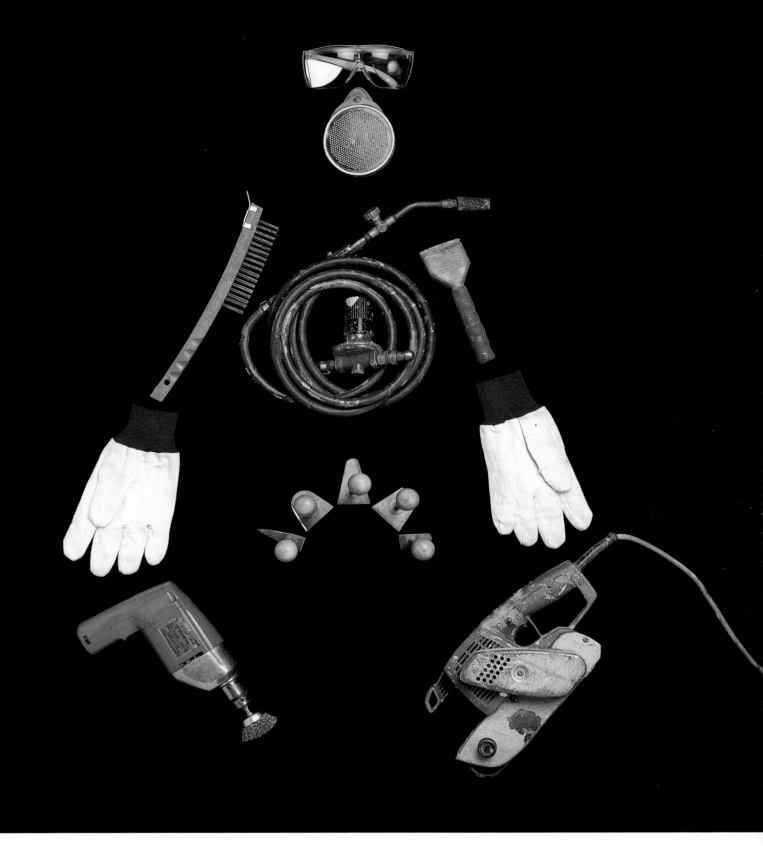

Man at work: basic materials used are goggles, mask, wire brush, torch, scraper, gloves, sanders, picks for scraping and filling. (DK)

trims, They're angled for neat, clean, easy edge cutting. Use them for touch-ups as well. Use 3-inch brushes for larger flat surfaces such as doors, fences, gutters, and steps, and 4-inch brushes for walls, ceilings, and floors. When painting clapboards, use a brush as wide as the clapboards. Use a 1- to 3-inch angle brush for corners, and small round or oval sash brushes for fine work or spindles.

Buy a wooden handle that fits your hand and has a sturdy ferrule (the metal strip that attaches the bristle to the handle) to keep the brush together. A good brush feels smooth and silky; it's resilient and balanced. A tapered edge fits into corners.

Hold the brush near the base of the handle. Don't bear down, but make the bristles flex slightly as you begin your stroke. Dip a third of the brush into the paint and tap gently on the side of the can. Apply paint with the tip of the brush, not the sides, in a steady, even stroke.

To clean brushes, use water, perhaps with mild soap, for latex paint; solvent or paint thinner for oil/alkyds. Hang the brush used for latex to dry. For a brush used with oil-based paint, brush the paint out, work the brush dry, then rinse it with fresh solvent or thinner, and squeeze it twice to dry.

True Faux: Fantasy Finishes

Grainings, marbling, and murals were enormously popular in the eighteenth and nineteenth centuries. Today's color designers are experimenting with new glazes and textures, using interior finishes on Victorian exteriors. Kits for glazing and marbling are available, but the result may look amateurish. With a little more effort, you can achieve professional quality results.

Trompe l'oeil. Trompe l'oeil, meaning "fool the eye," is a particular style of decorative finish that incorporates realistic or abstract images, perhaps as, or part of, a mural. It's usually classically designed to imitate architecture in places that are either too costly or impossible to construct, as in the cathedral ceilings in Europe. An element of *trompe l'oeil,* a fake window painted on a wall, for example, or three-dimensional-looking architectural ornamentation, such as an ivy vine or birds, is frequently used along with the following fantasy finishes.

Glazing: Sponging, rag rolling, and *stria* are three effects created by glazing. A glaze is the semi-transparent liquid that is applied over a "paint-ready" wall creating a textured, multicolored effect on a flat surface. Texture can be made with a sponge, a rag, a comb, a crumpled newspaper, etc.

Nicks and marks on wall glazes can be easily cleaned with a soft white liquid soap, such as Ivory, on a sponge. Touch-ups for more serious damage are simply a matter of dabbing a little glaze on the chosen texture-maker and blending it softly into the surrounding glaze.

Surface Preparation. Glazes start with a "paint-ready" surface. The walls must be cleaned, primed, patched, and painted in the body color of your choice. Wipe the wall or surface down with thinner or water before applying paint. This keeps the paint from drying too fast and prevents "lap marks"—the marks left when your wet brush overlaps the already dry paint.

Wall glazes can be executed in either oil-base or flat-latex paint. Which you choose depends on the technique you'll use. If your surface is base-coated in oil paint, your glaze must be oil. If the base coat is flat latex, use latex glaze.

For example, rag-rolling and *stria* (pronounced stri-áy) are more successfully done with oil paint because the paint doesn't dry as fast, giving you more time to manipulate the glaze to get the desired effect. Oil is better for kitchens and bathrooms as it is more resistant to the moisture buildup in those rooms. Always use gloves and a respirator when working with oil-based paints.

Sponging is best on flat latex because it dries in a flat finish, giving you a softer fresco look. Flat latex is water-soluble, making cleanup simple. Latex dries to the touch within minutes with little or no smell.

An oil glaze consists of a combination of a clear liquid such as McClosky's Glaze-Coat, semigloss oil-base paint tinted to the color of choice, and mineral spirits to thin the mixture to the consistency of heavy cream. A latex glaze is simply flat latex paint tinted in your desired color, thinned with water to the consistency of heavy cream.

The accompanying photographs show what glazes can look like on different surfaces.

Sponging. Paint the walls the body color. Mix three different glazes in dark, medium, and light tones. Have a clean bucket of water on hand. Different tools will result in different effects. A flat pop-up sponge gives a smooth, cloudlike texture. A natural sponge gives a more dramatic crunchy texture.

Christy Cizek, who specializes in creative *faux* finishes in San Francisco, recommends a natural sponge for the beginner because its larger size makes it easier to apply. She uses two 69-cent chip brushes bought at the paint store for applying the glaze onto the glazing sponge and blending color into the corners to create a smooth well-blended coverage. She uses a damp, clean, flat pop-up sponge to blend the edges of the glaze as it is applied.

Christy once turned a plain white wall into a blaze of sunset. She prepared the wall with a body color of warm white in flat latex. Then she chose a dusty rose

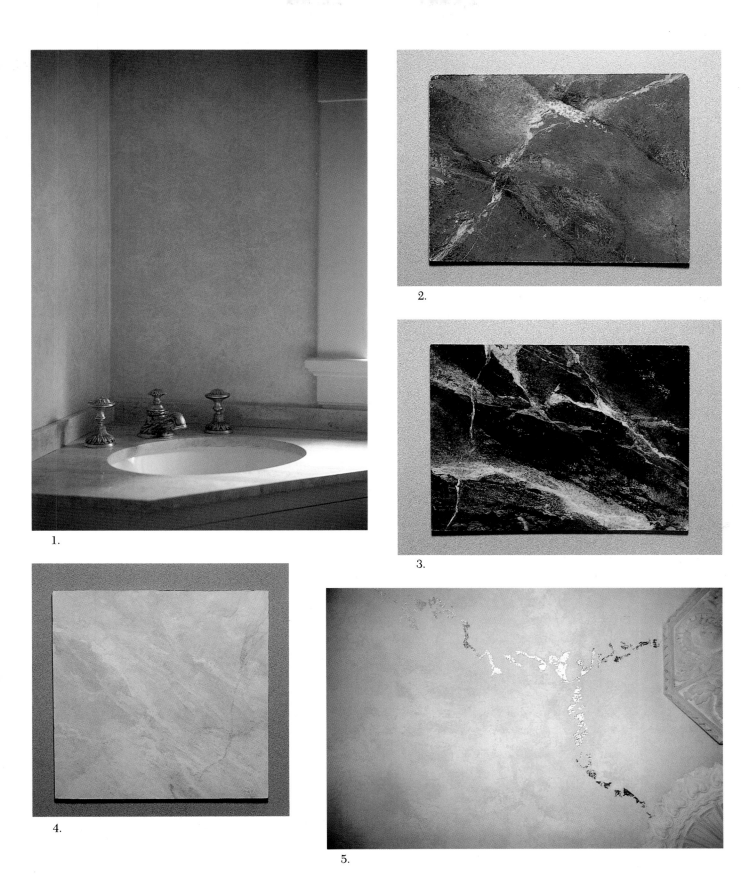

1.

2.

3.

4.

5.

These are samples of glazing done by Magic Brush. Number 1 is rag glazing. Numbers 2, 3, and 4 are examples of marbleizing. Each of these three examples has a different base coat and different choices for vein colors. Number 5 is rag glazing, using rag and cheese cloth for the finish and gold- and silver-leaf veining in a finishing coat of marbleizing.

Paul Kensinger of Color Quest used rag glazing to give a rosy glow to the walls of this gracious room.

with a blue tone as her darkest glaze. The medium glaze was a warm peach tone, and the light glaze was a yellow cream.

Starting with the darkest glaze, the dusty rose, at the highest part of the wall and working down, she applied two swipes of glaze onto a damp natural sponge. She quickly applied the glaze in a series of loose figure-eight motions, pulling the paint out in every direction until the glaze looked evenly distributed in the desired color richness. Then she patted the edges with the clean pop-up sponge, catching any drips or hard edges. She started the next application about a foot away, allowing the space to draw the new application of glaze into the previously finished section. She finished the entire room with the first glaze and followed with the second, medium, glaze with a little looser application, letting the first glaze to show through here and there.

Christy makes it a habit to stand back from the wall now and then as she finishes with the lightest glaze, to make sure the pattern is to her liking. For corners, she sponges the paint as close as possible to the corner and then uses a dry clean chip brush to blend the glaze smoothly.

She uses a bucket of each color and usually chooses three colors plus the body color, in dark, medium, and light. A bucket of water serves as the "clean" bucket. (With an oil-based paint, you'd use thinner or mineral spirits instead of water.) She uses a soft natural sponge in one hand, a clean crunchy sponge in the other.

Rag Rolling. A glazing finish similar to sponging, rag rolling is sharper and more "hard-edged" than sponging. It's a very eighties finish. When rag rolling, apply an (oil) alkyd base coat and let it dry, then add the glaze with a brush or roller. Thin with mineral spirits. While the glaze is wet, take a soft, clean lint-free rag, such as washed cheesecloth or an old T-shirt, and bunch it up in a loose ball. Roll it across the surface of the wet glaze.

The more pressure you apply, the more paint will come off of the surface. For a light airy look apply lots of pressure, but don't take off all the glaze. For a denser, more intense look, roll the rag gently over the surface, leaving lots of the glazing material on.

The accompanying photograph shows a member of the Magic Brush team at work, ragging a wall.

Stria. To striate, or comb, a flat surface, prime the surface, then paint on the base coat with an oil-based (alkyd) paint. While the base coat is drying, mix your glaze coat with an enamel oil-based paint in the color desired. Wait at least ten minutes until the surface of the base coat looks dull before applying the glaze coat.

Comb or striate through the glaze coat with a metal-toothed comb or instrument in any direction. You can even crosshatch or make wavy striations. You can comb the wall twice, overlapping the second line

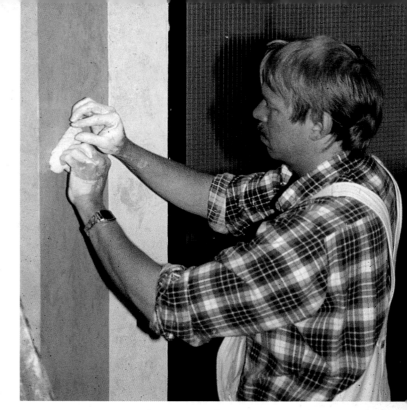

A member of the Magic Brush team is shown ragging a wall.

beneath with an adjacent comb stroke for another look. Wipe the glaze off the comb or instrument to prevent buildup. Christy Cizek prefers a special wood-graining brush with eight points that leaves eight evenly spaced stripes.

Irregularities are fine. Indeed, they'll help create the satiny appearance you're looking for. Let the glaze dry for twenty-four hours, then apply luster/satin varnish for protection.

To give you an idea of how to do things, we followed Christy Cizek, of FAUX, as she created a *striaed* wall.

Spattering. Spattering is the art of flicking specks onto a surface. Pretend you're Jackson Pollock. The wall or surface should be prepared with a base coat of flat latex in the desired color. Tape off the floor, carpet, or carpentry nearby, as this is a very messy project. Use a stiff-bristled brush on a small surface, a paint atomizer for a large surface. Dilute latex paint with water, and practice until it's a consistency that you're comfortable with. Wear thin rubber gloves. Let each color dry before spattering the next. Spattering gives a fun look, especially on porch floors. It's for any surface that needs a sense of humor.

If you spatter on a surface that has been striaed, the result will be *faux* stone. Moldings and woodwork around doors and windows are good candidates for a *faux* stone effect.

Feel free to experiment with other combinations of paint glazes. The accompanying photographs show the

a. Note that Christy Cizek always has two buckets, one with the paint or varnish, the other used as the "clean" bucket.

b. After painting or sponging on the base coat, Christy washes the wall with thinner to ensure a smooth base.

c. Then she combs the wall with her dark paint. Note that she is using an eight-pointed graining brush (rather than a comb) in one hand, and the sponge for cleaning up in the other hand.

d. Christy uses the sponge to soften the lines.

e. She combs, or strias, with the lightest color.

f. Again she uses the sponge to soften the lines.

g. To finish up and heighten the three-dimensional effect, Christy highlights the outer lines in the lightest color, using a small-tipped artist's brush.

h. Finally, Christy shows off a beautiful wall.

nonrepresentational (that is, it doesn't look like fake marble, or wood, or anything) glazing treatment on Robert Dufort's home in San Francisco.

Wood graining. Wood graining, *faux bois*, can be used to make any surface look like wood. Use a pale base coat—the wood color—and one light and one dark graining color. The base coat can be either oil or latex, but oil works better. For darker *faux bois*, apply it with a small wood-graining brush, available at artists' supply stores. Drag the thinly bristled brush across the wet glaze layer, wiggling your wrist a little for the iregularity in grain you're aiming for. Do one color at a time, first dark, then light. A brush with sections cut out of it also creates an unusual effect. Christy Cizek uses a special $26 artist's brush that has had chunks cut out of it at the head, and fuller rounds of natural bristle at the tip. Cork and rubber erasers can be used to draw in knots. Coat with protective varnish after the surface is dry.

Verdigris. Verdigris is a finish that resembles aged bronze or copper that has turned green. It is most successful on metal grillwork on gates, panels, or light fixtures. Prime your metal surface with a metal primer. Paint it in an exterior flat enamel in a deep brown tone. Choose a bright blue-green that is in the color family of the aging copper and thin it slightly. Then stipple over the metal surface, letting it catch in the corners.

Faux Marbre. Marbling, marbleizing, or *faux* marble gives a paint surface the look of marble. Any surface that can be painted can be marbleized. Jill Pilaroscia marbleized the columns on the Stick/Eastlake House as part of the color design shown in this book and used two kinds of marbling on the Mansard Home.

The accompanying photographs show several different kinds of *faux* marble on two of San Francisco's Painted Ladies.

Apply your primer and let it dry. Then paint the base color and let it dry. Then add tinted glazes in different patterns. Usually, you put one color of glaze over the entire surface with a natural sponge, and then trace irregular veins in a marble pattern of one, two, or three other colors, using feathers, erasers, rags, or brushes.

Christy Cizek's method for tricolored *faux* marble is similar to her glazing method. She chooses three colors of latex or alkyd/oil-based paint. She has a bucket for the dark color, one for the medium color, and another for the light, or vein, color. Then she crumples crisp newspaper into a fan. After washing the newsprint off her hands, she uses a natural soft sponge in one hand, a chip brush in the other. If she's using oil, she has a "clean " bucket of thinner; for latex, the "clean" bucket is water.

When the wall or column is ready and has been painted with the body color, she uses a clean sponge to wipe down the entire surface to make it smooth and damp. She quickly sponges on the darkest color, then dabs quickly with the clean sponge. Then she uses a slightly folded crumpled fan of paper, pressing it against the surface, pressing the wrinkles in the direction she wants the veins to run. Then she pulls the crumpled newspaper straight off. It will leave vein marks, giving it a cracked and shattered look.

She follows up with her medium color, mixed to the consistency of heavy cream. When the surface is dry, she drags the medium color across the surface with a 2½-inch or 3-inch chip brush, twisting the brush for a pattern. Drips are dabbed with a clean sponge.

When the surface is dry, she dips a fine artist's brush

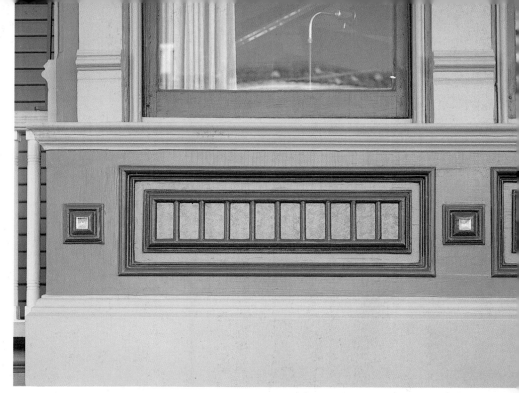

(Opposite). Robert Dufort's house.

Detail on the Dufort house shows nonrepresentational *faux* finish used for fun.

These are examples of *faux* marbleizing used on exteriors.

into the light color and sparingly, perhaps on a wet-again surface, drags it along. Using her lightest touch, she twists and turns the brush. Then she blots it a bit with clean sponge to break the perfection of the line. Now she has three different textures on the base color, and three colors, which creates depth.

As with all fantasy finishes used on the exterior of your Painted Lady, use two coats of exterior varnish after the design is dry, for a durable shine. One coat of varnish will peel too fast. Varnishing is the dessert and will make a *faux* finish look like it's worth a great deal more than the time and expense invested.

Ladders

There are stepladders, step stools, and extension ladders. If you use ladders, which are less expensive, less comfortable, and less safe than scaffolding, use the right ladder. It shouldn't be too short or too tall and should be at least high enough to reach to within 2 to 3 feet of the highest point. Read the directions on an extension ladder before extending it.

Both lightweight and durable, an aluminum ladder is best.

Lock the spreaders and don't stand on the top platform, the highest step, or pail shelf. Don't lean to the sides or overreach. Don't let the ladder tip. If there are doors nearby, either keep them locked or open them wide. The ladder angle should be 25 percent, or one-fourth, of the ladder length away from the house. For example, if you are using a 20-foot ladder, the bottom should be set 5 feet from the wall base. Make sure the top isn't near an electrical line, even if the ladder is wood.

Be sure that the ladder is level and use wood blocks for stability, if necessary. Move a ladder sideways by moving the bottom then sliding the upper end along the house. Don't leave a ladder unattended.

Lean the ladder on the unpainted surface and paint down, Keep the ladder from making marks by wrapping the ends with cloth rags.

Safety First

For a safe job, pay attention to these six safety concerns: Bees and wasps under the eaves or inside clapboard siding can be dangerous.

When removing asbestos shingles, wear face protection. The shingles can explode. For more information, call the Consumer Product Safety Commission: 800-638-CPSC.

Work in clean air with no flames or smoke.

Clean up as you work and keep containers closed when not in use.

Some paints contain solvents that can be toxic if inhaled, swallowed, or absorbed through the skin. Others can cause skin or eye irritation. Even if you are using the paint in the open air, you *must* read the safety warnings on the manufacturer's label before starting to paint. Those warnings will alert you to the need for protective clothing and will indicate whether you may need to use a respirator. Reading the label first will also protect you from making a mistake should you swallow a solvent by accident, or get it on your skin or in your eyes. It's best to wear long sleeves and pants, splash goggles, and butyl rubber gloves.

A need for respiratory protection is indicated by the words: "Do not breathe vapor or spray mist." While inhalation hazards are more serious when the paint is being used in a confined space, be aware of them even outdoors.

If you feel faint or dizzy, or begin to have a headache, stop painting for a while or use a respirator. (*Note*: If you need a respirator to keep from inhaling solvent vapors, don't substitute a simple dust mask! For respiratory protection from solvents, you need a cartridge-filter respirator, properly fitted and with fresh cartridges. Ask your paint dealer for advice.)

Follow label instructions for paint storage. Seal paint cans tightly and store away from sources of heat. If only a small amount of paint is left, throw it out. Don't store or reuse empty containers. Check federal and state regulations before disposing of toxic materials.

Have Heat Gun—Will Travel

Choosing the right contractor or color designer can mean the difference between a good job and a bad one—and between an experience you're satisfied with and one that can be torture for the duration of the renovation process.

Reputation and referrals are important, as are professional associations and licenses. Drive around town to see houses you like, ring doorbells, and ask who did it. Word of mouth is still the best reference. Ask contractors or designers for a list of houses he or she has done and check them out. Look at work that you are told is five or six years old and see how it has held up.

Make sure that the contractor and painters love Victorians. James Martin feels you have to love these buildings to paint them well. Personal relationships are important. You're going to be living with these people for up to three months, depending on the size of the job. Are they neat, positive, compatible? Do they share your sensibilities and goals? Use your intuition when you meet prospective workers.

Is the bid they make reasonable and complete? Too low a bid usually means the work will turn out badly. Who will be on-site overseeing the job every day, the contractor or a foreman? Organization is important. Get a commitment from your contractor that the job will be done straight through, with no stops and starts.

Put everything you can in writing. A sample contract will show you what you should, and should not, expect, both for the overall job and for the day-to-day work. It will cover specifics and procedures such as whether there will be spot priming or full priming. Agree on schedules.

There will be specifics, such as the repair of dry rot and other moisture problems, and reproduction or repair of woodwork and metalwork, that the contractor won't know about until after the priming is finished. Agree at the outset that the contractor will make that second inspection and that you must approve all corrective work before the house is painted. Don't assume that if something is not excluded in the contract that it means that it's included. If it's not written down, it's not part of the contract.

We've included the basic sample contract used by Gustavo Caldavelli, a Bay Area contractor. Use it as a guideline in making sure that all of your questions are answered before the work begins.

Although some color designers are also contractors, others just create color schemes. If they don't paint ask them for their recommendations. Ask them to oversee the color swatching on your house to ensure that the correct colors are used.

A color designer is a person who brings the vision of the homeowner together with the architectural integrity of the building. Color designers help owners understand their homes better and, at the same time, become more aware of their color preferences.

Often a homeowner will discover details that were hidden or unnoticed.

Don't hesitate to be frank about your likes and dislikes and your hopes for the building. And don't hesitate to ask why something is or is not picked out. Now's really the time to get to know your house thoroughly. Answering the questions in James Martin's questionnaire, in the adjoining box, will help, whether you're working with a color designer or doing the job yourself.

Questionnaire from The Color People

This is the questionnaire James Martin uses when working with clients by mail. Answering these questions is an excellent way for you to analyze your home and your feelings about it.

What are your feelings?

Your house should make you feel great every time you come home. Your input will help me create just the right look and feeling for your building. Please fill out this questionnaire. Feel free to use extra paper to express yourself.

1. What is special to you about your building?
2. What do you like about it? What works for you?
   - Colors
   - Architectural features
   - Balance
   - Windows
   - Porches
   - Detailing
   - Explain.
3. What do you dislike most about your building now?
   - Color
   - Balance
   - Style
   - Detailing
   - Size
   - Explain.
4. If it is your own home or office, describe yourself and your personal color preferences.
5. What impression do you want your building to make?
   - Dignified, refined
   - Whimsical
   - Lighthearted
   - Warm
   - Cute
   - Bright
   - Subtle
   - Other
   - Explain.
6. What are the main colors and feelings of the interior?
7. What colors on buildings elicit the most positive response from you? What is that response?
8. What is the building to be used for? What tone would the users like best?
9. What is the surrounding neighborhood like? What are the buildings next to it like? Are they close or far away?
10. What is the degree of detail desired? What about the brightness or subtlety of that detail?
11. What are your thoughts on colors? Any samples, photos, fashion, art, house magazine clippings, or the like that appeal to you and can help express the tone, color, or feeling you want will be most helpful.

Robert Dufort's Step-by-Step Guide to Painting a House

A subtle sense of humor and a bent for scientific research hide behind the twinkling blue eyes of this tall, lanky, soft-spoken Southern gent. Robert Dufort was born in Durham, North Carolina, in 1954 and studied psychology at Oberlin and Lake Forest. He moved to San Francisco in 1975, where his first job was working on fire-damaged buildings for a realtor. As he painted, he noticed the beautiful Painted Ladies blossoming in town, and he decided that he didn't want to do the fast-and-easy work required on speculative homes—he wanted to be involved in preservation and restoration.

A year later, Magic Brush was born. He quickly learned that the hardest thing for a painter who wants to do the best work possible is to balance that ideal against the need to make a living. He often worked harder on the job than he was paid for.

His marriage to Lara, and the birth of their son, Isaiah, brought out the businessman in Dufort. Now Magic Brush's eighteen employees, all specialists in their crafts, offer the highest-quality custom interior and exterior work. They specialize in structures in need of significant restoration because of paint-related problems.

Although they are known for their renewal and restoration of wooden Victorian homes, many of the buildings Magic Brush works on have been remodeled with new construction. When that happens, they try to make the old part like new, and give character to the new. For Dufort, performing a "painting restoration" assures that you are not just slapping a coat of paint over a building's problems.

His research and experimentation have led to the development of new techniques of restoration, which he shares with other professionals in seminars and articles.

Dufort's favorite customers are those who check out Magic Brush and then come to them for the best, people who know enough to tell the difference between companies and can afford it.

Since he won't know the extent of the repairs necessary until the prep work is done, Dufort bids or contracts for *knowns* only, although he does outline his assumptions in his agreements.

The experimental *faux* and specialty finishes Dufort has perfected, along with the unusual attention to restoration detail, led to Magic Brush's being awarded First Place in the National Paint & Coatings Association's "Picture It Painted" Award given for an interior in 1987 and 1988.

Dufort does marbleizing, *faux bois*, and verdigris ("pretend" wood and copper facing). His home on Beaver Street in San Francisco is the first to be embellished with nonrepresentational glazing on the door and panels.

Design-by-computer is next on the horizon. Using a PC-compatible computer, Magic Brush videotapes a façade or interior, feeds it into the computer, and then manipulates the image to test color, textures, and forms. He can even move furniture and create an imaginary room. Then he can take a slide off the monitor and print it, or transfer it to a floppy disk and make a print from that so a client can visualize a color scheme.

The major goal for Magic Brush is being responsive to clients. When Dufort wields his magic brush, run-down white elephants become cherished Painted Ladies.

Doing It by the Numbers

Painting is the easiest part of creating a Painted Lady. To explain this paradox and give Victorian homeowners an idea of the many details that have to be considered in creating a Painted Lady, the following section describes the painting and restoration of 1198 Fulton Street, one of San Francisco's finest Victorians.

Not all buildings need the same things, so we have also included photographs taken of work by Magic Brush on Robert Dufort's own home, an Italianate with an Edwardian second floor and gable.

Basically, there are five steps to creating a Painted Lady, whether it's a woman or a building:

Shower—or power wash
Tone—scrape and sand
Powder the face, or prime the building
Paint—redden the lips, highlight the eyes with mascara
Top it off with jewelry—the gold leaf

1. **Inspecting.** Before you take the first step, look carefully at the house.

All paint jobs should begin with an analysis of the existing conditions, followed by a plan of action. A new paint job rarely fails because of the paint; it usually fails because underlying conditions are not properly treated.

Check all the surfaces, using binoculars if necessary, for hard-to-reach areas. You've already decided on

1190 Fulton Street when finished. (DK)

your color design and chosen your painter or contractor. Make a list of the steps needed to prepare your home for painting. Determine your priorities:

What are the worst areas?

Which will take the most time, money, and energy?

Which areas should be torched or chemically stripped—and where can you get away with scraping and sanding? The front may need everything done to it, but you may be able to save time and money on the sides and back.

Will new carpentry work be necessary?

A house can be in bad shape without sheets of paint falling off it. Look for signs of paint failure such as blistering, bubbling, and peeling. They indicate moisture that's trying to get out of the building, leaks, or intercoat failure. "Alligatoring" or "crazing"— cracks and peeling—may mean that the oldest layers of paint have dried out before the top layers and aren't holding up. Moisture problems have to be corrected. Most old paint will have to be either stripped or prepared to hold the new layer of paint.

Estimate all paint costs and contracting specifications, along with the number of days to be spent on each job, before you proceed to step 2.

Another planning break should be taken after the first priming, because it's only then that you'll be able to assess where the dry rot is; which nails have rusted and need to be replaced; whether the sheet-metal facings on gutters, chimney caps, and downspouts need replacement; and what woodwork needs to be replaced or repaired. Solve the problems, don't just paint over them.

2. **Scaffolding.** Although ladders and rope-and-pulley falls are less expensive than pipe scaffolding, they're not as safe, not as easy to use, and make the job take longer. Ladders over 24 feet long are not recommended for DIYers (Do-It-Yourselfers). Scaffolding for the front of a three-story house on a 25-foot lot can cost as little as $400 to $500. This picture shows the scaffolding on 1198 Fulton near the completion of the job.

3. **Sealing.** Seal the house. Close the windows and seal them with towels, if necessary.

4. **Washing.** The first step on every job is to wash and clean the building to remove accumulated dirt, mildew, fungus, chalking, and rain salts, all of which interfere with the adhesion of paint. Power washing is the preferred method, particularly on larger jobs. Compressors force water out at 2,000 psi (pounds per square inch). Compressors rent for about $50 a day and a small Victorian can be washed in a day.

Scrub with a soft plastic fiber brush. If the building has a lot of mildew and fungus, spray the infected area with a three-to-one solution of water and normal household bleach or chlorine and let it sit for a bit before washing it off. Detergent can also help in removing dirt. You may also use a chemical injector attachment to add bleach to the washing process.

Let the house dry. Overnight is usually adequate.

Although the power wash can remove peeling housepaint, that's not its job, and you can hurt the wood if you "wash" too hard and force water into it. The power washer can develop pressures up to 3,500 psi. Protect yourself as well as your building. Use a mask or respirator, especially when working on lead paint.

5. **Stripping.** Stripping with heat or chemicals is next. "Burning is like shaving your face. The tool has to be very sharp. The paint is like the hair, and the wood is like the skin, so cut closely but leave no burn spots—no nicks, so the surface is left smooth and silky." Gustavo Caldavelli of Cal Crew Painting is one of the San Francisco professionals who uses a heat torch with a live flame for stripping old paint. Torching is the most effective but the most dangerous method of removing

Close-ups of bay-window panels showing alligatoring. (RD)

Scaffolding is assembled. (RD)

old paint. It's a most delicate process, and one not recommended for weekend painters. If you choose this method, you must get a permit.

The painter bubbles the paint with the heat torch and then shaves it off the house. The finished surface doesn't have to look brand-new, however. It's okay to have leftover paint in the pores—you're preparing the surface for an application of new paint. You aren't shaving off the skin, just the surface hair. As a safety measure, buy inexpensive latex caulk and fill the joints and cracks and holes before setting the flame to wood. It works very well.

Never point the torch up, because the flame goes up—and that starts fires. On a curved shape, work sideways. Never burn anything that hangs over the torch parallel to the ground. Use correct burning tools with big, medium, and little nozzles to accommodate different-size moldings.

Whether you use heat or chemicals, be sure to use the correct scraper for the job. Make sure it's sharp.

The Old-House Journal recommends a heat gun, which is heavier, harder, and slower to use. However, used properly, it can be much safer than the torch method. As with torching, fire is always a danger, so wet down the wood, especially around cracks and joints. Heat can get into crevices and behind moldings and windowsills. Wet surfaces down before using heat for stripping. Do a small area at a time, then stop and hose it again after scraping. Keep the heat moving. Heat rises, so work from the bottom of the house to the top. This will make the job easier as you go along.

On flat surfaces, use a heat plate. This, too, is heavier and slower. You lay it on the flat surface until the paint is "cooked," then scrape off the paint. After a while, you'll be able to heat with one hand while you scrape with the other. Keep a hose on hand and be careful when you hold the torch away that you're not burning something else, such as a bush.

The use of chemicals to remove large areas of paint is on the rise. This technique is used more in the East than the West, and also more commonly used on stucco and masonry surfaces than on wood. The efficiency of chemical stripping is not what it should be, particularly with heavier buildups of paint. Chemicals are very messy as well. Since state laws differ, talk to your local professionals and paint store personnel, test a small amount before committing to a large purchase, and follow manufacturer's instructions to the letter.

For safety's sake, wear goggles or safety glasses, a respirator, protective gloves, and long sleeves. Change clothes after work and wash before eating.

6. **Sanding.** After the house is stripped, most surfaces have to be sanded. In areas where the paint does not have to be totally removed, scraping and sanding are usually adequate. The most common tools are putty knives, which are pushed, and paint scrapers, which are pulled to remove loose paint.

After the paint has been removed, most surfaces require a light sanding, either by hand or with a small electrical orbital sander. It's light, can fit into all but the smallest spots, and can even handle most trim work. The sander buzzes and vibrates and is used to dull glossy surfaces, sand down imperfections and paint residue, and soften the line where paint has been removed. What you're doing is preparing the surface so that the paint will adhere to it. It should be clean and smooth, but not so smooth that the paint slides off.

An electric belt sander may be used on large flat surfaces such as siding. This is a large, heavy, two-handled machine. Surface damage and fatigue can easily result from using this sander improperly. Work carefully. Don't forget to use a dust mask.

Different power sanders and different kinds of sandpaper are required for different jobs, from #50 grit—a very coarse sandpaper—to #600—which is as fine as paper. Painters normally use #60, #80, #100, #120, and #220 for perfect enamel finish work on the trim or door ornament.

Avoid circular sanders. They move very fast, but can leave swirl marks and gouge the wood.

7. **Inspecting.** Now go back over the house again. Inspect for problem areas, for loose or missing trim. Are the plaster capitals and moldings such as egg and dart in good shape? Check the sheet metal flashings around the roof, chimney caps, and gutters to be sure they're water sealed, secure, and rust free. Check the putty on windows to be sure it's tight. Check the wood for dry rot and rust spots and be sure window joints are secure. Now's the time to check the roof. Specialists may have to be called in to analyze and correct certain problems.

Now is also the time to be sure the moisture problem will not reappear after you've painted. You can mix a mildewcide in with your paint to keep mildew from returning.

For loose trim, it's sometimes easier to remove the trim, and fix it or replace it, then reattach it to the building.

Rust spots on wood are usually caused by rusting nails. The nail should be pulled out and the dry rot around it should be dug up or plugged up with epoxy or wood-resin fillers. Renail or screw in another hole, as necessary. Countersink the new nail cap with putty or caulk to eliminate the bleed through or use galvanized nails.

Dry rot is usually caused by moisture, although termites may be a factor. With dry rot, the wood softens and deteriorates until you can stick a pencil right through it.

Dry rot can be found on windowsills, between trim joints, and around rusted nails.

Torching. (DK)

Heat plate in action. (DK)

Torching. (DK)

Heat gun in action. (DK)

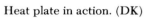

Orbital sander at work. (DK)

Belt sander at work. (DK)

Dry rot, rusted nail. (RD)

Remove the loose, "punky" wood fibers and rusted nails. After renailing and securing, drill small holes into the end grain (the end of the piece of wood, not the flat side) so you can inject the two-component epoxy consolidants. This product is absorbed through the wood into the affected areas, where it kills fungus and encapsulates the wood fibers, stiffening them to allow acceptance of the patching material. If the area of dry rot is very large, it can be partially filled with pieces of wood.

For bigger holes, use epoxy patching material, which comes in two tubes that are mixed thoroughly together, then applied with a putty knife. After the epoxy cures, or hardens, the epoxy patch can be easily sanded, filed, or shaped. The epoxy fuses with the surrounding wood and flexes at a similar rate to wood, producing an almost permanent repair.

These epoxy-consolidant and epoxy-patching materials for wood can be purchased by mail order from Abatron Company and Smith & Company. Other epoxies can sometimes be found in marine supply stores. BONDO, a low-grade polyester resin, which is almost as good, is cheaper and can be purchased at automotive supply stores. It's harder to mix but easier to mold into shape. Epoxy can be used before and after priming.

Spackle and similar powder compounds sometimes recommended by paint stores are not recommended for wooden Victorians because of their limited flexibility. Caulking is preferred to spackle because, like wood, it will move with the wood and take normal stress. Another epoxy-like product, ABC, replaces dry rot with spray and is good for windowsills and wooden stairways. You spray three times, allowing it to dry between each spraying.

8. **Priming.** Applying the first coat of primer is the next step.

Priming serves as a foundation for the paint. It ensures good adhesion between old paint, bare wood, and the finish coats of paint. Spray on the primer, then work it in with brushes. Prime from top to bottom.

You'll have to choose between a linseed-oil base, an alkyd exterior primer that penetrates the wood, or an acrylic. If all the surfaces are clean, deglossed, and well prepared, the acrylic primers are better because they're more flexible. But if the building has chalky surfaces, then an oil/alkyd primer may be the better choice.

Additives such as emulsifiers, mildew inhibitors, and tints will help the primer work more efficiently. If you're using one coat of primer, tint the primer lighter than the finish coat you plan to use. If you use two coats, make the first coat off-white.

9. **Caulking and Puttying.** Caulk, whether it's latex or paintable silicone, is a flexible material in a tube that you squirt into seams and joints with a caulk gun. Elastomeric, a water-soluble resin mixed with latex that's extremely flexible, is recommended. After injecting the caulking with a gun, smooth it with your fingers, then go over the surface with a wet cloth to be sure no excess is left.

Remember that not all seams should be filled with caulk, as it is important to leave ways for moisture inside the house to escape. The seam found between each siding board and the one above is a good example of where not to caulk. Caulk any seam that will allow rain to enter your home.

Use putty for nail holes. The rule of thumb at Magic Brush is that they use epoxy if the hole is bigger than a dime, putty if it's smaller.

10. **Prepping Windows.** Make sure that the glazing, another kind of putty, next to the glass is smooth, clean, and sealed. Prime the edges around the window and the windowsill.

To protect the glass while working, use a plastic masking tape like Visquin, which is 1 millimeter thick, and mask all the windows so that all the openings are covered. The plastic tape won't allow paint seepage and won't hurt the glass.

Remove the shutters, then fix them, paint them on both sides, and reattach them after the house is finished.

11. **Fixing Trim.** Replace missing trim or add new trim. Sometimes it's more expensive to repair woodwork than replace it. Victorians frequently dressed up their homes by ordering frilly borders from mail-order catalogs and tacking them onto their houses. Mail-order catalogs still offer lacy woodwork and trim in any style for every surface imaginable.

12. **Priming Again.** Use a second coat of primer on stripped and new wood.

Naturally, you'll concentrate less on the back of your house or a light well than on the front. Sand hidden areas with a power tool and prime at same time. Then fill in and paint quickly.

The façade will be your pride and joy. Sand the second primer coat to make it smooth. Gustavo Calda-velli says, "If you love your house as much as you love your wife, you'll use #120 or #150 sandpaper on the whole house to provide the most perfect finish."

Then dust the house with duster and damp cloths with a solvent in them to pick up all the dust. "Then you're ready to paint, " Gustavo says, "that's the easy part."

13. **Swatching.** Use small portions of the paint you have chosen to paint a section of your house to be sure the colors work both on the house and with each other. This is your last test. Look at the paint for a day, in different

Dry rot before repair. (RD)

Dry rot after repair. (RD)

Dry rot before repair. (RD)

Dry rot after repair. (RD)

Wood-consolidant repairs in progress. (RD)

After prep work, but before priming. (RD)

lights, from morning to dusk. These pictures show a color swatching of one bay section of 1198 Fulton, along with the finish coat of paint. When Robert was discussing colors with the owner, she told him he could do anything he wanted so long as there was a touch of chocolate brown on the house. It's on the panel molding.

14. **Finish Coating.** Painting the finish coat on a house is the easiest part of Painting a Lady. It's also the most gratifying. You see results immediately.

The finish coat you select will depend on the exposure to the sun and the surface being painted.

The body of the house will have a flat or satin finish. Trims, windowsills and sashes, and architectural details will have a semigloss or high-gloss finish. Always use whatever sheen seems most appropriate. Use different paints for the house, the steps, the railings, the brick or masonry foundation, the wrought-iron crown, and the cast-iron fence.

Magic Brush prescribes 100 percent acrylic paint. Dufort feels that the key to longevity is flexibility. The joints on wooden houses move, expanding with the sun and contracting with the cold. With acrylics, the thicker the paint the better the flexibility. The reverse is true with oil/alkyd-base paints. He recommends one coat of light paint if there's enough coverage in the paint; two coats of darker paint, if it's a southern exposure. If the budget allows, Dufort prefers two-and-a-half coats—a quick third coat on the still tacky second coat so you apply less paint the last time around.

Paint the flat body areas with a brush, roller, or spray. When you spray, "lay it off"—go over it again quickly—with a hand brush while the paint is still wet. Magic Brush also sprays the main trim first to fill in most angles, then "cuts in" the remaining colors and cleans up the line where two colors meet.

Spray distributes paint evenly so it looks better. You should work the paint in with a brush, however. But you have to be very experienced to use a sprayer, since the paint has to be even all over. The smaller the opening on the tip of the spray gun, the more atomized the paint and the finer the finish. A 15,000 to 17,000 tip is preferred for finish coats. DIYers should not use airless sprayers because the spray can penetrate the skin. An experienced painter can do the best job with spray paint, but only if the paint is "laid off" with a brush, in the direction of the wood grain.

If you're not experienced, use a brush. For acrylic paint, use a 4-inch polyester brush for the siding. Paint in the direction of the wood grain. Use the same size strokes. Be careful not to leave brush marks when you put the brush down for the next stroke. Brush softly so you leave no marks.

If you're doing it on your own, apply accent colors to the house, working from top to bottom, with a day between each color.

Always paint from top to bottom, and on smaller sections, from inside out. First inside the door, then the windows and sashes, then the trim around the moldings, then the outer trim.

A full gallon can of paint is too unwieldy to use, so divide the paint between two cans. Seal the one you're not using to keep the paint clean and ready.

Take care not to paint the lawn, the bushes, or your neighbor's car.

15. **Accenting.** Color accents, polychrome, is what makes a Painted Lady. Color code your trim colors to make it easy to follow directions when you're painting. For an example of how to do this, look at David Irvin's rendering. Use high-gloss paint. Different moldings and colors will demand different brushes, from 1 inch to 3½ inches. On some trim, you may need to use angled brushes.

Paint every coat from top to bottom. Do the first color from top to bottom, and then the next day do the next color, top to bottom. Some painters put one paint over the edge a little and then cut a sharp line with the next color to be sure that the whole house is painted and protected.

On 1198 Fulton, six colors were used, along with the gold leaf accents. There were 120 gallons of acrylic/latex primer and 80 gallons of 100 percent acrylic finish coat used. The job should last ten to fifteen years. A repainting in eight to ten years should require half the time and money, since only spot priming will be needed.

Attention to Details

Several parts of the house will need special attention:

1. **Varnished Doors.** For a natural wood-finish door, strip it with varnish remover using a soft brush in all the corners. Then wash it with a lacquer thinner such as trisodium phosphate (TSP), a salt that neutralizes the effect of the varnish remover, and let it dry. Give the door a light sanding with #180 paper—always with the grain, never across the grain—then apply one thin, even first coat of color stain on top. Again, let it dry.

Spar varnishes, the kind used on boats, are recommended, in a solution of 50 percent solvent, 50 percent varnish for a thin first coat. Let it dry overnight. The next day, sand with #180 sandpaper, until all the shine of the varnish is gone. Dust with a brush, then a Tac cloth, which will remove all the dust and static. The second coat should be 25 percent solvent, 75 percent varnish. Again, apply a thin coat and let it dry overnight. Then apply a thin coat of 10 percent solvent, 90 percent varnish. Let the door dry where it won't get dusty, and sand with #220 paper. If desired, dust with a Tac cloth

Bay section showing color swatching. (RD)

Bay section with finish coat. (RD)

Robert Dufort swatching his house on Beaver
Street. (DK)

Beaver Street house, almost finished, but
before gilding. (RD)

Finish coats. (DK)

Bay-window panel after priming. (RD)

Bay-window panel after painting, with four colors on this small area. (RD)

again, and then apply a final coat of 5 percent solvent, 95 percent varnish.

Pure varnish dries too fast. With solvent, you won't get brush marks so the finish will be smooth. Use a soft horsehair bristle brush. Two tips: Don't overload the brush to save time—it won't. And don't let the varnish run. You'll end up with a smooth, polished, well-stained door.

2. **Steps and Decks.** Wooden staircases, decks, or porch floors, will always peel eventually because of the constant stress and flexing, but you can create a good-looking deck that can last a decade. First, replace all the nails that have become loose. Brass screws will stand up better to the constant moving, and you want the structure to be tight.

Since movement on steps and decks will be constant, aim for a flexible coating; it will last longer than a hard one, which will crack rather than bend. Robert Dufort recommends (1) epoxy paints, the kind used on docks; (2) a sealer that's half epoxy and half sealer coat; (3) or an elastamatic coating such as Geco Deck, which goes on in three coats.

Balustrades, banisters, and other wood trim on the stairway may have to be replaced or repaired. These pictures show the front staircase balustrade handrail being replaced by master carpenter Erik Kramvik.

3. **Metal.** Metal, such as pipes, should be cleaned, scraped with a wire brush, and primed with red oxide primers. Treat rusty metal with a rust converter such as Extend by Duro or Rust Destroyer by Advanced Protective Products. Brushed on, it reacts chemically with rust to form a tough barrier that locks out future rust.

4. **Stucco.** Stucco must be power washed, sandblasted, or chemically stripped, not burned.

5. **Bricks.** After checking the mortar and replacing where necessary, acid-wash bricks with muriatic acid, scrub them with ammonia, then wash them under high pressure. Transparent sealers or colored paint will seal and protect brick.

6. **The Entryway.** The front entryway is the first thing people see when they walk up to your home. Pay special attention to the door, windows, interior ceiling of the porch or portico, and woodwork.

On 1198 Fulton, the massive front entry portico columns, once cast iron, demanded extra attention. These pictures show the front entry portico column being prepared and patched with epoxy.

7. **Bay Window.** The three photos on page 43 show the stages of prepping and painting a bay window at 1198 Fulton. The first photo is a close-up of the upper bay

window area with ornamental woodwork and alligatoring paint. The next photo shows how the same area looks after being stripped by torching, after initial priming and caulking. The third shows how six colors, highlighted by gold leaf, glisten.

The Finial

The wonderfully graceful topnote shooting up into the sky from the topmost point of the house, or portico, is the finial. Some homeowners use weathervanes as finials.

The house on Fulton had rooftop finials above each bay and a grand finial atop the tower. The grand finial is a huge structure, subject to great stresses by San Francisco winds, which can reach 80 miles an hour. It had to be partially disassembled, and resecured by climbing inside the tower roof and bolting it to the roof timbers.

The decorative metal vanes were set into the wooden finial body and base. The vanes were heavily wire brushed, treated with a solution that converts rust to an inert organic compound, treated with rust-inhibiting primers, and then painted.

Gold Leaf

Gold leaf is the last thing you put on your house. San Francisco color designers are again one step ahead of the rest of America in adding a new fillip to their designs: the lavish use of gold leaf to highlight rosettes, finials, and small but important bits of gingerbread. Although the cost of painting a large Victorian can be daunting, the use of gold leaf is economical.

Sheets of 22-karat gold leaf are available at sign shops, major art supply stores, and well-stocked hardware and paint stores. A little book of about 24 pages, each about 3½ inches square, costs about $30 to $40. Each page contains three to four thumbnail-size pieces. Each sheet is only 1/100 inch thick and is usually "patented," or attached, to a thin sheet of tissue paper. Gold leaf without the patent, or thin separating sheet, is cheaper, but is harder to use. There are several different kinds of gold leaf, including German, which is a yellow gold; Italian, which is red gold; and Japanese, which is white gold. A "golden" gold leaf is made by the Swift Company in Connecticut.

Giusto Manetti Goldbeaters of Florence, Italy, have been selling gold leaf since 1820. Theirs has a favored luminosity and depth of color. A 25-leaf packet, 3⅜ x 3⅜ inches, sells for less than $2 a page, and you can press up to eight finial or rosette tips from each sheet of gold leaf.

Applied properly, gold leaf outlasts paint three to one, or fifteen to thirty years.

To apply, start with a thin coat of Spar varnish or sizing to the surface you plan to cover. Allow it to dry

Front staircase balustrade. (RD)

Front-entry portico column before torch and epoxy repair. (RD)

Front-entry portico column after torch and epoxy repair. (RD)

Bob Behling prepping front-entry portico column. (RD)

The newel-post finials were missing entirely, so new ones were designed by Erik Kramvik and then turned by Gail Redman Woodworks. (RD)

The grand entry doors were in poor condition. Here painter Tyrone Stewart works with hand tools.

The door trim consists of
many small pieces. (RD)

This is how the finished door turned out. (RD)

Bay-window ornaments after torching. (RD)

Bay-window ornaments after priming. (RD)

Bay-window ornaments finished in six colors and gold. (RD)

Bay detail before prep and prime showing a previous restoration attempt that damaged the wood. These pieces were then duplicated, primarily on a lathe at Gail Redman Woodworks, and then assembled and installed by Erik Kramvik. (RD)

Bay detail after prep and prime, showing restored woodwork. (RD)

Finished bay detail. (RD)

Main finial during prep. (RD)

Main finial during painting. (RD)

Main finial completed. (RD)

Erik Kramvik repairing finial base. (RD)

Bob Behling setting restored finial in epoxy. (RD)

for perhaps half an hour, until it's sticky or tacky, that is, about 95 percent dry. Then slide a sheet out of the packet and place the gold leaf side of the sheet against the surface to be decorated. Use a fingernail to tamp it off gently but firmly. In other words, you're putting the gold leaf on as you pull away the tissue paper. You'll end up with a blank sheet of tissue paper and a shiny rosette. Don't seal or cover the gold with varnish to protect it because that will cut the sheen of the gold in half.

Some painters apply a *boles* finish sizing under the gold leaf (the red you see in these pictures). The *boles* hides the "peekaboos" and amplifies the gold's color. The *boles* can be mixed into the sizing, but sizing takes several hours to dry to the proper point of tackiness and many painters prefer a fast-drying lacquer.

This is the most satisfying part of the job: putting the jewelry on your Painted Lady.

After you finish the work, have riggers remove the scaffolding so you can see your new Painted Lady.

Now all you have to do is celebrate a job well done!

Before gilding. (DK)

Sizing. (DK)

Applying gold leaf. (DK)

Applying gold leaf. (DK)

Tamping down the gold leaf. (DK)

Touching up the gold leaf. (DK)

The gold leafing is completed. (DK)

Riggers dismantling the scaffold. (DK)

The Magic Brush crew.

Portraits of Six Colorists

In putting together *How to Create Your Own Painted Lady*, we asked six of the best-known color designers in America to share their ideas for designing Victorians and their philosophies on color.

The six colorists are Californians Jill Pilaroscia and Bob Buckter, who are based in San Francisco, and Doni Tunheim in Santa Cruz; James Martin in Denver; David Irvin in Fort Scott, Kansas; and Joe Adamo, formerly of St. Louis. With the exception of Jill, the work of all these colorists appears in *Daughters of Painted Ladies*.

They share three things in common: (1) For all of them, being a color consultant was an accidental profession. (2) They are all passionate about using color to make Victorian architecture sing. (3) Each of

the six looks at the use of color in exterior decoration differently, yet they all share a contemporary viewpoint.

Although several of the designs would have been at home on any nineteenth-century street, the attention to detail and shading as well as the choice of colors make their designs right for today's homeowners.

Jill Pilaroscia and Bob Buckter, along with Robert Dufort, Erik Kramvik, and Gail Redman, whose handiwork appears in the step-by-step section, are members of Artistic License, a guild of highly talented San Francisco Bay Area professionals who are in the forefront of the American resurgence in Victorian arts and crafts.

JOE ADAMO

"My technique is playing with light. I frequently choose two colors that are real close to each other, and I expect the light to work with me. At dawn, midday, and dusk, the light plays tricks and works with the colors. My work is subtle, not candyland like San Francisco."

Joe Adamo, Victorian artist and "Mad Colorist" of "the Gateway of the West," left a crowded color market in San Francisco for St. Louis in the late 1970s, where he "found a little pocket and has been going right down the street." He has turned enough row houses, some of them condemned, and purchased for $10,000, into proudly shining town houses to transform Lafayette Square into a thriving area of the city. If the house has a color scheme that got passersby excited, or outraged, chances are it's a house that's been painted by Joseph E. Adamo.

With his broad, sweeping mustache, tiny gold earring, and dashing straw hat, Adamo is the only color designer we know who could go to a Halloween party and find two people in costume complete with mustache, disguised as Joe Adamo.

Born in Brooklyn in 1942, Adamo wrote poetry and sketched in Greenwich Village clubs while getting through Bedford Stuyvesant's Boys High. He was doing watercolors and oils, and loved it, but he couldn't make a living. The rest of his family extolled the benefits of civil service. Then one day in 1969, he got

into a car with three friends on his way to Florida. "We made a right turn near Washington, D.C., and landed in San Francisco."

He had painted interiors in Brooklyn and found a job working with house painters. One job with three friends, called The Marx Brothers, taught him spraying, block and tackle falls, and teamwork. Bob Buckter gave him some jobs and showed him how to use a spray machine. He went on his own, dividing his time between San Francisco and St. Louis, where his wife's family lived. It took three to four years before he found a homeowner who let him be creative.

While he was living as a single father with his three- and four-year-old children in the Mission district of San Francisco, he painted his landlady's house on 24th Street as his rent. She wanted traditional American Indian colors and chose red, yellow, turquoise, and black. Adamo explained that the colors were too basic, they wouldn't work, and he picked charcoal, a toned-down red, her turquoise, and her yellow, changing the value, not colors. She wasn't happy until he did a test portion. Adamo painted the 24th Street house himself, leaning down and reaching up from a 40-foot ladder, and his artistry was immortalized in the mural painted on a nearby wall.

Back in St. Louis in 1981, cars lined up on Whittimore Street to see each new paint job, and Adamo soon had more work than he could handle.

JOSEPH
ADAMO
Victorian
Artist
color consultant
231-9240

CAUTION!
KEEP FROM FREEZING

(Opposite). Joseph Adamo, Victorian artist.

(Right). A St. Louis door created by Joseph Adamo.

(Below, and below right). Adamo house on 24th Street in San Francisco, with detail shot.

Most Victorians in St. Louis are Second Empire, tall and narrow, made of brick or limestone, with detailing on the cornices and over the windows. The façade is usually done in soft colors, with bright accents at the top, around the windows, and on the doors. Adamo's doors are so colorful a St. Louis gallery sells a poster of "Adamo Doors."

"St. Louis houses focus on the façades, so you can do more faster."

As he said in *Daughters of Painted Ladies* "A house is like a giant canvas and I like to accent every detail. A carpenter didn't hand-carve an intricate rose so that it would be lost in a solid coat of paint."

Adamo sees himself as an artist, chemist, carpenter, mason, tinworker, and painter. Craftsmanship and authenticity are his main concerns.

And he asks his customers whether they want colors that are busy and excitable or muted and calm. He feels his work can enhance the beauty of the building, and bring out its best. "I meet with the people and tell them what it looks like it needs—besides paint. Everything is repaired, especially the wood moldings and gingerbread, even the copper gutters. If the customers want shortcuts, they don't get Adamo."

He is the only colorist-painter we know who guarantees his work for five years and offers annual follow-up preventive maintenance for the next five years.

Limestone does tend to fall apart with age, and when it releases gas, it can bubble the paint. Touch-ups can save a Painted Lady from premature aging.

But thorough prepping, stripping all the old paint off, is crucial. He power washes the limestone, sandstone, and concrete buildings, using a biodegradable paint remover. The chemicals are rolled on, left for twelve hours, then power washed, which takes four or five hours for the whole façade. When the paint is all off, he follows up with a deep-soaking masonry sealer that is the primer. He also uses ready-made epoxy that fills and seals hard and is guaranteed for ten years. Filling, caulking, masonry, and carpentry repairs follow, before a finish coat of 100 percent acrylic paint.

To Adamo, quality is most important in choosing paint. In St. Louis, where temperatures can range from over 100 to minus 50 degrees, paint has to be durable. Acrylic paints have more elasticity and can survive a harsh climate. They won't alligator, shrink, and break like oil-based paint will. Adamo likes Porter and Devoe color palettes, since he likes working with subdued, muted colors. He's partial to Porter, a local paint company, because they offer individual big 6-by-3-inch swatches, rather than a fan deck.

Adamo recommends a seimigloss finish. It's easier to keep clean. Gloss brings out all the defects under the paint; a flat finish hides a multitude of sins. In sunlight, a glossy wall will be flattened out, while it will be glossy in shadow. Semigloss offers the best of both and has the best fade factor.

After meeting with his clients, Adamo gives them books of color decks to help them decide on colors. When they know the kinds of colors they want, Adamo chooses colors and color tests on the building so the paint can be seen throughout the day, and he and the client can think about it. "Sometimes there are arguments between husband and wife. They may have different ideas. I tell them take a week, take what you need, to decide. It has to last you ten years."

He selects the main color, the wall color, first, then selects trim and up to five accent colors. Usually he works in six to eight colors. There are so many different lines and layers on each building, and each part should have different color.

For one six-story business building downtown, Adamo prescribed twenty-one colors—but the colors graduated so slowly from grays into mauves into wines into purples that the lines of the building were needed to delineate the colors properly.

Adamo goes back and forth, testing each corner and using the whole house as a canvas. The gradations in the cornice molding can change while the rest of the façade is being painted. One of his favorite jobs is the Autumn House in St. Louis seen in *Daughter of Painted Ladies*. He was painting it as the leaves were changing in the park across the street, and with every change of color, Adamo mixed new colors, making new colors to harmonize with the fall foliage.

To get a good paint job, Adamo offers three rules: "First, preparation is the most important thing. If you don't do that right the rest won't hold up. Second, if you decide to hire someone, look at the painter's buildings. Regardless of recommendations or qualifications, see what he's done. Ask questions. And third, when you do it, after all those years, keep it up. Don't let it run down again. Maintenance pays for itself.

"I take my customers on their fantasy. They have to be satisfied. That's my main objective, regardless of whether or not I'm satisfied with it." Adamo remains amazed at the range of color and its potential on exteriors. In 1988, he moved back to San Francisco for a while, looking forward to new challenges.

BOB BUCKTER

"Rare beauty is what I seek in this world, and if I can't find it, then I try to create it." From his sparkling blue eyes to his Madras plaid shirts, Bob Buckter lives color. Buckter has created color designs for more than 1,500 Victorians from New Orleans to Australia. And it is a source of pride to Bob that no two of them are exactly alike.

Buckter has done more than 300 houses in the outstanding collection of Victorians on the small island of Alameda in San Francisco Bay. He also consults on commercial non-Victorian buildings and on neo-Victorian complexes springing up across the country.

Born in 1946, Buckter is a second-generation San Franciscan. He studied business and social sciences at City College and San Francisco State, then started studying for an MBA because he always wanted to have his own business. Now he uses business and psychology in working with clients and running BB Color.

Buckter's first job was painting a house by himself for $1.85 an hour. On his second job, his pay was raised to $2.30. Two weeks later, he put his own house-painting ad in the now-defunct San Francisco Progress. Then his rate escalated from $30 a day to $100 a day, and he hired painters from the union, who taught him the trade.

In 1971, Buckter put his first color design on an Edwardian on 17th Street. He had seen the work of colorist Butch Kardum around town and decided to do a four-color job. After it was finished, a friend painted a sign for him to put on the house. The sign led to other jobs, other signs, and all the work he and his employees could handle. "This is a pretty free-spirited town," Buckter remembers. "Anything goes, everyone lives and lets live as long as they don't disturb the next guy."

Like a badge of honor, each newly painted house proudly displayed a sign hand-painted to match the house and, through the brushes of Bob Buckter & Friends and other colorists drawn to the challenge, San Francisco's Painted Ladies blossomed. "It was hard to do at first," Buckter recalls, "and I did a lot of experimenting. I was determined to be a master at this, and I wanted to create work that pleased people."

Sometimes Buckter carried 200 colors of paint in the back of his truck to test with before deciding on a scheme for a house. And when his parents went on a vacation, Bob and his brother Don, who restores and paints houses, painted the family house in seven colors. "They came back and couldn't find their house. They didn't appreciate it for three weeks, but the neighbors loved it. In 1985, we changed the whole palette again.

And they couldn't find it again—and it still took them a while to appreciate it."

By 1977, the painting-contracting business was in the black and Buckter asked one of his co-workers, color consultant Tony Canaletich, to manage the company, and Bob sailed around the world on a windjammer. When he came back, he found ten to fifteen outfits specializing in painting Victorians and decided that the glory and the fun was in the colors. Now, although Buckter still has his painter's license, he just consults and then recommends painters.

Buckter believes that "like so much in history, color goes in cycles. Two centuries ago, Colonial Williamsburg was decorated with bright, clear, fancy colors. You can see them today in Mount Vernon, George Washington's home, which Matt Mosca has scientifically researched and restored. The desire for those colors has been up and down ever since. To me, the palette of 200 years ago is now more relevant than the Victorian palette."

When working with homeowners, Buckter begins by defining colors. He juxtaposes some of the 300 to 400 colors on cardboard "brushout" cards he carries around in his overstuffed briefcase. This gives him a sense of his clients' tastes and color preferences. He may also show them a portfolio of his best jobs and a copy of Painted Ladies.

He tries to gather all the decision makers together at one time. Clients explain what they like and don't like, and Buckter looks for any pattern or relationships in the architecture, then asks what their favorite colors are.

Bob also gets reactions to what's next door, around the corner, and around town. At the same time, he picks up overt and covert signals by seeing what clients wear and how they live. Then he suggests a few basic colors to test their reactions.

Buckter feels that there are two schools of design. In the first, the consultant finds out what the clients' likes, wants, and feelings are, then chooses colors to reflect their personalities and the design of the house. Buckter believes that a good color design reflects the client.

The second approach to design is the cold approach. The designer comes in and tells you what you should do. This design reflects the designer, not the client. But some people really don't know what they want and want to be told, which makes things more difficult. Buckter will then give recommendations on colors and where to put them.

This approach also works with designs by mail. Bob asks for fifteen or twenty photos showing various trim elements and configurations of trim, then numbers the

Bob Buckter with his two joys—his house and his car.

Queen Anne house in New Orleans. Color consultant: Bob Buckter. (DK)

Bob Buckter shown working on his color design for the Embellished Queen Anne house that is illustrated on page 97.

paint chosen on the photos and includes a sheet of recommendations and colors to correspond with the numbers. Then the painter can "paint by number."

When working with an actual house, Buckter has the painter test the colors on a small area of the house after the house has been primed, a practice he heartily recommends.

That's important to do before buying huge quantities of paint or turning a painter loose and ending up with a job that looks bad. You can't appreciate all the effects of light and the juxtaposition of colors on a house by just looking at little color swatches.

Buckter frequently uses a white tone, such as bone or oyster (never *white* white) to trim Victorians with a lighthearted touch. Some historians insist that an authentic color scheme would use dark trim, although light trims have been authenticated.

He prescribes white tones for all horizontal sills, which are frequently sheet-metaled. The surfaces perpendicular to the sun receive the maximum dose of ultraviolet light and the more the sun beats down on a surface, the worse the wear is. So the lighter these surfaces are, the longer the paint lasts. This way, the whole building will weather at the same rate. So a white accent is useful as well as cosmetic.

How long a paint job will last is an essential consideration. A San Francisco building facing north will last about ten years; five years if it faces south. A paint job with poor preparation can start to break up in two years.

Naming the brand of paint as well as the colors is important, because several paint companies may have the same name on their color charts, but since they have different formulas, the colors are different. For example, Hunter Green is on at least three charts—and it's different on each one.

Bob has found that "color hangs there in space until it's next to another color, then it creates a place for itself. The key to understanding color is juxtaposition." He makes up color cards, large pieces of cardboard painted with colors he uses, many of them colors he has created, and he puts one next to the other, next to the other, next to the other.

Chips can't tell the true story. They can't tell how colors will "telegraph" on the whole exterior. Brushouts on the building prove to the client that the design works.

By this time, however, Buckter can juxtapose the large brushouts from his briefcase and show people what the colors will look like together.

"I make a big fan in my hand and say, 'Here's the main body and major contrast trim. Then we'll use little bits of this with this as the accent.' To see different grays, I show people a monochrome of grays. There can be five different ones, from light to dark: Oyster, Gray Fish, Ozark, Chimney Sweep, and Charcoal.

Then we look at a gray-green with the same values. Or a gray-violet with the same value as Chimney Sweep.

"The Grand Mariner gray is lighter than Mississippi Delta and Sorcery is lighter than Mississippi. But they're all monochromes of gray-violet. I mix colors, and if they work together in my hand, I know they'll work on the building.

"And I remind them that outdoors, colors will be more intense. But if a house is always in shade, it won't look as bright as it might in the sun."

Once a color palette is selected, Buckter narrows down the selections to juxtapose colors and placement, from the main body to smallest accent. Frequently, the house will say what colors it wants to be. Having the architecture to work with is half the battle. The main body color is most important, then the major trim, then the accents, the eyeliner, and the gold leaf. "Ninety-nine percent of the time it works."

His design for Bay Meadows Race Track won Buckter the Second Place Commercial Institutional Award from the National Paint & Coatings Association. There were so many additions in varying architectural styles, it was hard to bring everything into one focus. So Buckter used seven colors, along with frieze boards stenciled with horses and racers and a lot of graphics, to pull it all together. He made the graphics the focal point and not the architecture and created a new image, a new illusion. "Creating a new mood—that's what art is all about."

In 1975, Bob Buckter & Friends painted San Francisco's historic Mish House, a freestanding house that appeared in *Painted Ladies*. All four sides were painted twelve colors for about $7,000. Buckter used aluminum paint on a house for the first time to get the silvery finish he wanted. He also used burgundy automotive finish because he couldn't find anything that would produce the quality of color he wanted.

For example, the color burgundy usually has no opacity, no "hide" or "coverage," which means that three coats are usually needed to cover what's underneath. The automotive finish was more expensive, but it worked in one coat.

A pure white has no "hide," either. So Buckter pigments it by throwing in a bit of raw umber, which provides a lot of coverage.

Buckter creates colors because he can't always find what he wants in manufacturers' palettes. By creating his own, he can supply the demand from customers and also control the fade factor. "I've mixed other colors and grayed and muddied and lightened and darkened and shaded and tinted and added different colors to others from different paint companies. Paint companies now keep track of the colors I've designed.

"Once I've found a color I like, I go to the company with a color-base system I trust, such as Benjamin Moore, Martin-Senour, or Fuller O'Brien. I work with a color base such as Blue, Red, Bone, Green, or Purple, start with that base, which is factory-ground, and tint in. Painting with color-base systems costs more but ends up saving the homeowner money.

"When I use Fuller O'Brien's factory-ground pure colors, Ultra Blue, Green, Red, Yellow, Black, and Purple, to shade or mix, the new color will have a great "fade factor"—even the blues and yellows.

"Clean, pure colors can be too intense for most people, unless they're only used as accents. Many clean colors and pastels are also semitransparent. They have no opacity or coverage so you have to use three coats instead of one. Since you have to have 'hide' for a successful paint job, I add a touch of lampblack or raw umber to a clean color to give it coverage and make it last." Buckter is always searching for ways to make paint last.

"Some colors can 'twinge' people. One client in San Francisco, whose house will appear in *The Painted Ladies Revisited*, wanted his house to look like a circus wagon—to be so bright you could see it around the block. I used Ultra Yellow stepped down with a touch of white and a tiny bit of dark pigment for coverage, but it turned out to be a real polarizer—either you love it or you hate it. And with pure purple and Ultra Dark Blue and gold leaf, the whole house is an accent."

There are two phases in designing color, Buckter notes. The first is the color design itself, choosing which color goes where. The second is the specifications sheet he gives to the painting contractor. This spells out the names of the paints, the colors, brands, formulas, sheens, and placements. Buckter feels that the color values, their intensity, and their placement are equally important.

Buckter feels that homeowners working on their own should start with telephoto shots and then follow his seven-color prescription for a successful color scheme:

1. A medium color value for the main body in a satin (low-sheen) finish.
2. A light color value for the major trim. White or a white tone such as bone or oyster in semigloss for window casings, sills, fascia, columns, pilasters, columnettes, dentil blocks, cornice brackets, and balustrades.
3. The minor trim—window sash, panel molding, frieze, borders—in a dark value, with a semigloss sheen.
4. A primary accent with an intense color used sparingly, in any value, with a flat sheen.
5. A neutral "backgrounder," usually a medium-dark value, perhaps as a window sash, to act as a neutral catalyst for the accent and minor trim. This neutral backgrounder is a noncolor that you don't really see but it helps everything, makes everything else work. It isolates and accentuates the other colors.

It soaks up other colors so that the intense colors that make color designs "pop" are effective.
6. For fun, a secondary accent that contrasts with the primary accent.
7. Gold or silver leaf or another special effect. Silver doesn't hold up as well as gold, but Buckter has been experimenting with aluminum foil for his next dazzling final touch.

Balance in placement is vital, especially when using accents. Buckter suggests a string of accent running either vertically or horizontally on the face of the house—not both. "Restraint is very important in the design of anything. There's always a risk of overdoing it, a law of diminishing returns.

"For example, a little oboe in an orchestra is tasty. But if it steals the show or overrides the rest of the instruments, it is too much. You should want more of it but can't have it. It's an emotional response. It's hard to define why a bit of color is tasty. Why you want to eat it up. But it can become too much."

Buckter recommends that after the homeowners have chosen the designer and painter they feel they can live with for the next few weeks or months, they should try to be sure the contractor will do the right amount of preparation.

Determine how much deferred maintenance is possible and what's really needed. If your house faces north and is surrounded by trees, you may not need major prepping after twenty years. (If your house is out in the sun facing south for thirty years, you won't need major prepping because there won't be any paint left on the wood!) Normally, a house should be repainted every ten years, so lots of stripping is needed.

If you're going to paint the house yourself, you have to know how to sequence your paint. To put polychrome on a building all at once, put on one color. Then "rag it off to the edge" where the next color goes. That is, use a rag to wipe the edge of the paint stripe you've just put on so it's smooth and even. Then put the second color on in another spot, and rag it off, then repeat and repeat until you've finished that level.

By that time, the first coat is dry where you've ragged it off, so you can put the fourth color on, and so on. You can also use your finger—in its glove—to rag off a color for a clean edge, so there's no bleeding or mixing of colors. The ultimate artist's brush is the fingertip. Fingertips dot rosette tips and anything else that needs just a dot of color, such as gold leaf, better than anything else.

One of Bob Buckter's most innovative color designs was for his award-winning handmade, 1955 Mercedes Benz 300-S Cabriolet. After totally restoring the car, Buckter chose a a ripe dark aubergine for the body and then used one part aubergine with one part Shiny Ultra Black to achieve a seductive tone of purple-black on the body of the car. The perfect finishing touch is an accent graphic that suggests a running board.

Bob Buckter wants to transform the whole city. There are still unpainted Victorians in San Francisco, and colors he hasn't been able to persuade people to use. "Yellows are just now coming back in popularity, at least as an accent. Pinks have been out for a decade. I have brushout colors I call Dusty Rose, Pale Red, or Dark Rose, even 'Snuggles,' but no pink. Bright green is too much for most people, so I used it on my own house on 20th Street. There are thirteen colors on my house—including another color no one else will accept: Ultra Purple.

"I like this job because it keeps me thinking. I like people. I like to figure people out and match colors to them. Art evokes an emotional response. When people look at my work, I want them to feel a certain way that reflects my clients, usually happy, but it can be somber. It's different every time. That's why it's fun."

DAVID IRVIN

"When I was a kid, I loved playing with blocks. I still love to play with my kids' blocks and Lego games. And when I look at a house, I strip everything off and envision it as a big heavy dark box or a fairly light box—then I build up or down with other blocks of colors as if each trim board has its own color."

David Irvin is an architect and designer in Fort Scott, Kansas, once a frontier outpost where the Oswego Indians lived peaceably next to the settlers until the 1870s, when railroads cut through the land and made Fort Scott a bustling frontier town of 25,000. Now there are only 10,000 people, and Irvin, the only architect, has led the way in obtaining federal grants to restore the downtown area.

Born in Omaha and raised in New Jersey, Irvin was in Kansas City for his senior year in high school. His project in drafting class was a model of one of the houses created by visionary architect Bruce Goff, a friend of Frank Lloyd Wright. Irvin knocked on Goff's door, introduced himself, and was guided by the master during his studies at Kansas State University. There he met his wife Janet, who was raised in Fort Scott. Their girls, Kelly and Betsy, are four and eight.

Irvin was interested in the use of color on exteriors but could never try it until he discovered a copy of *Painted Ladies* at Woodlawn Mansion, George Washington's stepdaughter's home in Washington, D.C. The Downtown Rehabilitation Project offered Irvin the chance to implement his ideas. There were forty-five buildings, all needing rehabilitation and restoration, sidewalk-canopy construction, and signage. The project also required innovative techniques to keep costs in line. Irvin helped the town meet preservation guidelines and conform to federal grant requirements. He created a Victorian theme to bind the downtown area together, and at the same time meet the needs of individual building owners.

The Department of Housing and Urban Development granted federal funds to help, but it was a voluntary loan program and no one signed up for six months. Then they saw Irvin's three-color transformation of the Hurst Asher Corner Drug Store. In three months, Irvin had more applications than he could handle.

But people still needed to be encouraged to use color. "People would look at a building and say, 'I don't know whether I like that or not.' I'd say, 'Let's try a sample,' and they'd say, 'Yeah, I like it.' Then people started painting their own houses, with or without our help, in pinks, greens, and reds. Of course, we could never call pink pink. We called it rose, dusty rose, ashes of roses, peach, sand, anything but pink."

Irvin was experimental, flamboyant, or conservative, depending on the building. His company did masonry repair and restoration, rejuvenation of brickwork, surface preparation, and exterior painting and design. When the energetic architect discovered that the W. F. Norman Company, which had created the best tin ceilings and cornices and brackets in the 1890s, was still in business and only twenty miles away, Irvin helped restore Fort Scott interiors as well. The town is half Victorian, half contemporary, and it's all being designed in a unifying way.

Most of the buildings are masonry and sheet metal, with wooden window frames. Sometimes Irvin painted the brick red before tuck pointing (fixing the mortar). Sometimes the paint was removed to expose the original brick color, if it could be done without damaging the brick.

As with the other colorists, Irvin believes that correct preparation is the key to a good paint job. He recommends careful sandblasting of metal surfaces such as the cornicework and power washing the masonry with biodegradable chemicals. After all the loose or old paint is stripped or scraped off, he specifies a prime coat and one or two finish coats, balancing the

David Irvin in his own Painted Lady.

David Irvin's home in Fort Scott. (DK)

customer's budget with his vision of how a building should look.

After working on his own Victorian home, he enjoys bringing others to life. Irvin feels that frilly detail needs light. He believes that Victorians thrived on individuality. And he tries never to repeat himself in a color design. Houses speak to him, telling him how they feel.

His company usually provides clients with whole-house renderings and sketches of blowups of the details, whether he's helping local people or working through the mails. Irvin flies his own small Cessna to nearby states to meet with clients.

For the Buchanan County Courthouse in St. Joseph, Missouri, he restored the exterior from the ground to the tip of the dome and renovated the interior, adding modern touches. The final result was true to history and a striking restoration. The Powers Museum in Carthage, Missouri, was also an effective mix of history and modern convenience.

After removing the 1950s metal siding on the Union Block in downtown Fort Scott, David rebuilt the exterior as simple planes, so that the brackets and cornices could be easily added later when the budget permits. The canopy of the Office Supply Store is attached to the façade with chains of large lipstick-red "paper clips."

He always tells clients to buy one gallon of each paint first, before they buy twenty-five gallons, and he tests for the owner's—and his own—satisfaction. For out-of-town clients, he recommends brands and colors and comes out to talk directly to the painter. He can prescribe completely or work with the painter verbally. And he always specifies colors by paint brand. Since most of the painting is put out for competitive bids, he tries to ensure that the colors are matched correctly with the paint brands he specifies.

"On our house, we spent $100 on gallons to test with. We had three tones of blue—dark, light, and lighter. Then a buff trim, and red, dark postal blue, and pink on the door. We had to do quite a lot of restoration. Whenever a detail—a spool or spindle or dentil—fell off, the old owner would just throw it over the nearby cliff. 'He wasn't a preservationist,' said a neighbor. But at least I could find enough bits and pieces to have every piece of gingerbread replaced."

Most of the time, he chooses Pratt & Lambert paint because he likes their color system and deep accent colors. He also likes picking colors from their warm color palette poster and cool color palette poster

hanging in his office, then leafing through the books for specific shades. The really dark colors he uses are also from Pratt & Lambert. He also uses Sherwin Williams paint.

When he can't find the matches he's looking for, Irvin mixes two colors so they're the same color in different depths or shades.

For Do-It-Yourselfers, he suggests first asking whether you want a light house with a dark trim or a dark house with a light trim. Irvin feels that it's hard to make a mistake if you stick to historic color charts.

One technique is to use complementary colors, opposite each other on the color wheel, which make each other look more vivid—blue opposite orange, for example. If you want to make each color less vivid, toning each other down, then use supplemental colors, those next to each other on the wheel. The trim with siding could be complementary. Tones of the same color can be supplementary.

Irvin feels that there is more fear of color than use of color. People have fears of going over the edge of good taste, so they end up being too conservative.

"Don't overanalyze color by trying to get a perfect match or comparing minutely different shades of gray. Colors will always look different on a house from the way they do on a chip.

"I ask my clients what color they would like to start with as a base, such as blue or green. They rarely have opinions about detail colors, and that's where I can help most.

"I just tell people to stay away from fluorescent colors or metallic ones. Stay away from OSHA, safety orange, that stuff the yellow line in the middle of the road is made of. Use colors that are bright, but found in nature, not chemically created colors. Flowers are colors. No one ever says, 'That's a terrible-looking mum' no matter how bright it is. I like the crispness of good contrast in colors. You can't have peach and peach next to each other, so we just add another color for contrast.

"I really like color and want it used. I'd like to explore lavender. The deep reds and plum spectrum. The colors used on these six houses show 'my true colors'— I had carte blanche and had fun with them.

"Architecture is a passion. Creating something out of nothing, exploring new forms. I find real pleasure in taking old buildings and reviving them and making people enjoy them again—it's a joy to bring a building back to life to be appreciated."

JAMES MARTIN

"Color has been the hallmark of the 1980s. It's something whose time has come. Youth, success, attainment, and fun are all associated with our infatuation with color. People want color. They want it on their persons and in their homes. Now they want it on the outside, too—even on ten-year-old tract houses and sparkling new postmodern skyscrapers.

"The color *Zeitgeist* and the public infatuation with Painted Ladies are driving the final nail into the coffin of the Bauhaus mentality. People want a little pizzazz and individuality with a sophisticated, up-to-date approach. People can and do judge a house from the curb and color is the first thing they see. There's nothing I like better than taking a 'dog' property and making a beauty of it."

James Martin, Denver's "Color Wizard," has a reserved, natural, almost Downing-like approach to color. He uses subtle gradations of natural stone colors, tans and pinks and grays.

He founded Restoration Graphics in 1980, while working in the construction end of renovation. As The Color People, Martin's firm specializes in exterior design and architectural color consulting. His designs take into account the architectural history of the building, its locale, and the tone or image the owners want to project. A preservationist, Martin is a member of Historic Denver and the National Trust, and is the founder of Colorado Preservation.

To Martin, Denver is a young city whose emotions are near the surface, as befits its Western heritage. "The city is alive; its mood is volatile, ranging from the gloom and doom of depression to the exuberance of a conquering hero for whom nothing can go wrong. In Denver, like no other city, emotion, mood, and Western culture are recorded in its architecture, from the log cabins of the winter of 1858, to the brick and cottonwood palaces of the placer mining boom the next year. The architectural evidence of a boom-and-bust cycle up until the Silver Panic of 1888 can still be seen on Denver streets."

James Martin was born in Oregon in 1945, and grew up in the Northeast. He studied industrial and graphic design at the University of Bridgeport in Connecticut. His teachers were protégés of Josef Albers, the artist and master colorist at Yale, who preached that color and the use of color were everything.

As a student, Martin studied the effects colors have on each other. "When you put color A next to color B, both colors can change, and change even more when you vary the background color. On a building, this means that you can use the body color on the cornice and by surrounding it with the right background color, make it appear to be a third color, saving both time and money."

"What I do is not that fancy. I've looked at how color works on buildings for nine years. In 1979, everyone in Denver was going crazy, trying to do colors, experimenting with jillions of quarts of paint. I saw what was missing and what worked. I did exterior colors in summer, carpentry indoors in winter. And went national with mail-order color design in 1982."

In the beginning, Martin had a friend who painted his house gray. It looked okay, but not great, so Martin suggested, "Why don't you paint the front door red?" Suddenly the house came alive. His friends were ecstatic and he discovered a new business. "Anybody can do a gray-and-white house. The things that people miss are the accents. They come in with a conservative color scheme that won't look too bad, but it would look great if they'd just add a little color somewhere.

"A coral pink trim. A periwinkle blue window frame. A raspberry red front door. Roof lines, doorways, chimneys, and windowsills are great places to experiment with color." He likes softer colors for the body of the house, which fit most houses better, and he avoids color trends.

When he can meet with clients, he tries to learn their likes and dislikes. He leaves a book of hundreds of photographs, many of them from Denver, including all kinds of architecture so they can better identify what appeals to them. "It's like taking a trip around town at home."

Martin doesn't think of potential colors for a building until he's met a client or seen dozens of photographs and an owners' "essay" on their ideas for the house.

Photographs of all sides and details of the building and a questionnaire describing the clients' desires and budget; the given colors, such as roof tiles and base; and the locale and landscaping all help Martin select colors.

We've included a copy of this questionnaire on page 21. Whether you're working with a colorist or on your own, what you learn by filling it out will help you.

Martin then makes sketches choosing paint colors, usually from the more than 1,600 colors available from Benjamin Moore. He uses a shorthand that is now used by other designers in specifying paint. *B* stands for body. *B-1* is the primary body color and *B-2* is the secondary body color. Trim and punch colors can also be primary, secondary, and tertiary, and read *T-1, P-1,* etc. Trim colors are those chosen for the gingerbread or structural trimming on the house, while punch colors

(Opposite). James Martin and a client.

(Above). Queen Anne house in Denver with color design by James Martin.

(Below). A typical color swatch by James Martin, showing how he weights the colors even on the swatch.

are usually small bursts of intense colors chosen to add an accent or special sizzle to the design. Sashes must be painted, too, and they are S-1 or S-2.

His aim is to make the house look whole, using color to minimize any architectural defects in the building, bringing out its best. "Paint can make something too prominent recede, or vice versa. It can balance the house. The home becomes a statement of a complete environment that is the reflection of the owner."

His clients receive photographs and renderings of details of the building, marked with instructions for the painter and a 2½-by-5-inch board of color samples ready to bring to the paint store. On the board, Martin has attached color chip samples of the chosen paint in swaths, or strips of color, with the main body color being given the widest strip and the punch color being given the smallest. Specific placement and paint numbers are on the back. A sample is shown on page 65.

Martin suggests that the client paint a prominent part of the building first with samples of the paint so the colors can be seen at all times of the day.

The entrance can be the focal point of the house because it shows you where to go in—and color can direct a visitor's attention to the door.

"The tone or style statement of a building, whether it's dignified or whimsical, is the most important thing. And color is an inherent factor in setting that tone. Colors, bold and daring or subtle and complex, are being seen in interiors and exteriors. Color can make a fashion statement, can add texture and variety to a building, and can show off the best of the building. In the proper hands, color can make a heavy stolid building look lighter, or create a feeling of substance on a building of marginal character.

"As a preservationist, I frequently get asked about the historical authenticity of the colors I use, and I'm beginning to think that sometimes authenticity isn't all it's cracked up to be. Colors and placement can have a historical basis, but the house doesn't have to look musty.

"I don't know how many people I've met who treat their Victorians like children. None of my clients who, after asking for a historic paint job, has, upon seeing and authentic Victorian color palette and paint scheme, found that that is what he or she wanted.

"For most people who live in old houses, authenticity is of small concern. They love their homes and want them to look nice, usually with today's touch of colors. They live with color. And also live and care for their own house. They practice what they preach. The point is not that the house is a museum piece, it's that you've kept the house for posterity, and you've protected it well for the future.

"Victorians had so much exuberance. They had conquered the world and were so proud of it, showing off with everything they could accumulate, that Victorian clutter. They wouldn't just have chosen yellow ochres and browns if they could have used our colors.

"At the same time, the building must retain its architectural integrity. Too often, overzealously Painted Ladies become more details than house, and the original proportions of the building are lost. Porches, dormers, and bargeboards should not be allowed to jump off the main body of the building. This will happen if colors aren't closely related or if the contrast between the parts and the whole is too great.

"Detailing is back with a vengeance. We pick out details better than the Victorians did. I think that this is because now we live so much faster than they did, we need to bring out details so people will stop to see them. Also, we're glorifying things we'll never see again."

For Martin, there are four rules for making your house look good:

1. Work with the "given" colors such as the roof, bricks, stone, and foliage.
2. Always use a top brand of paint and check the color chips and samples outside in daylight before buying it.
3. Use a light color for window sashes.
4. When painting broad areas, get the most visual return for your money. For instance, areas with relief should always be painted a light color, so that the natural shadowing enhances the relief—and you won't need an extra color to do so.

"For example, I used light colors on sculpted lines on the Stick/Eastlake house so the shadow becomes another color, a color that changes and gives the house more of a dimension. With framed-in soffits, everything will shadow. Use a soft, light, rich color on a column (not white-white, which will just glare) and the Corinthian capital, then the shadows will bounce around and pick up light.

"This is also a money saver. For instance, instead of painting the dentils, use a color that's light enough to shadow, so you don't have to accent it. Then you save money when the dentils are accented by the shadow. Also, you can spray instead of doing it by hand. For example, I can spray a cornice a light soft color like gray or cream. Then when I put maroon next to it, the color of the cornice actually changes to look like a third color—a visual mix between the maroon and the cream.

"It goes like this: Take a row of dentils and the bed mold behind it and the crown mold on top. Paint it all one color, maybe with spray. Darken the crown mold, which plays up the shadowing of the dentil.

"In another instance, with soffit, crown mold, bed mold, and set of dentils: Spray it all a light color like cream; and then, painting by hand, cut in the crown mold in a dark, rich color, like burgundy. The cream-colored dentils take on the burgundy reflection and you end up with as much detail for half the price. The dentils are still called to attention, yet you've saved yourself another painting step—and money."

One of Martin's pet peeves is painters who exaggerate the difference in cost between three and five colors. "If you are going to use a punch color in the sashes, the dentils, and the finials, there is no more material or labor used except for a few minutes to clean a brush to paint each a different punch than to paint them all the same color. Why should you pay more for that?"

He also feels that the house should fit into the fabric of the neighborhood. A loud house could sing in Cape May but be horrid in Cincinnati because it's out of context. Even a building that works in Colorado Springs won't work in Denver. "What you do should fit the world the house is in. Otherwise, it's like wearing a fancy ball gown to a barbecue. You'll be seen all right, but not appreciated. People want to be noticed, but they don't want to stand out. Pretty colors aren't enough. It's like having lots of treble and no bass."

He also has to remind people that what's on paper isn't what the house will be like. A client in Manitou Springs, Colorado, complained that the colors chosen weren't strong enough. Yet when the house was finished, the final accents, the bass notes, "made it all sing out."

Although Martin has clients in twenty-two states, he rarely has the chance to use ten or twelve colors in a design, and he misses the richness of San Francisco's architecture—the houses with "jillions of details."

"Working in person can be much nicer than by mail because you get to meet people and that can be fun. Otherwise, you don't get to know the people as much as you want to. And you're doing something that's really personal.

"I like to have a house make a statement from the road. I want it to have an initial statement to make and another when you're close up to it, so you get the perfume. I like to put little things there so you really have to notice, subtle things, things you don't see until you live with the house for a while before you see that there are surprises."

JILL PILAROSCIA

"I always need fresh blood. I have an eclectic collection of paints and colors I've mixed myself. Nothing is sacred. I use anybody's chips. I go into paint stores and collect chips. I also use fabric, leather samples, photographs, and magazine clips. It's too limiting to stick with one paint line. There may be only six examples of neutrals in one company's fan—and if I can't find it in a sample, I make it up.

"Today, the human eye is more accurate than the computer for custom color matching. I mix all my colors, and usually, the eye catches the true color better than the paint store's computer can, especially on deep colors, which can be pretty complex. Did you know there are over three dozen blacks in Japan alone?"

Jill Pilaroscia develops colors for a fabric, leather, and lacquer manufacturer. She also works on flooring colors for commercial clients and teaches color theory to interior designers. She's on the alert for trends in color in interior design, always testing and experimenting with new colors and color textures. She uses *faux* finishes on interiors and exteriors, including marbles, wood grains, Zolatone, or flecked paint, for texture.

She and her husband, Jack Carroll, a union shop painter for high-end residential and commercial buildings, named their three-year-old daughter Emerald. Their son Blake is eight.

When it comes to working on exteriors, Jill has learned that architects often feel threatened by colorists and that painters are sometimes adamant about using the brand they prefer. So if she can't control the paint, she can and does control the colors by mixing her own—and eye-matching on the spot.

Jill was born in 1949 and grew up in Rochester, New York, with a father who would plant an acre of dahlias in all colors just for the joy of it, so she loves big swaths of color.

In 1973, Jill graduated from the San Francisco Art Institute with a degree in painting and drawing. At a time when photo-realism was hot, Jill did big abstract color-field paintings, which were considered too weird, too out of fashion.

So when she saw an ad in the *San Francisco Bay Guardian* that read: "Person to paint large areas of color," she answered it. The ad turned out to be for a housepainter for Bruce Nelson of Local Color. It was an all-male crew and Jill had to do anything the men could do on the scaffolding. Four weeks later, Nelson's colorist quit, and Jill was a colorist. Her first job, on Noe and 19th Street, symbolized what she calls her "ketchup-and-mustard" period.

"Winning first place in the Painted Ladies contest at the San Francisco City Fair was the turning point of my career." She was in a field with all men, such as Bob Buckter, Tony Canaletich, Butch Kardum, Jazon

Jill Pilaroscia mixing colors on-site.

A Jill Pilaroscia Architectural Colour
creation in San Francisco. (DK)

Wonders, and Robert Dufort and she felt she had finally arrived. "Bob Buckter was my idol. He said the same thing to me then as he does now. 'Shoot from the hip and do it quicker.' So I went out on my own."

"I've swatched schemes from the very beginning, mixing colors on the site. It's a different approach and it's my credo. I give lots of personalized and ultracustomized service in which the client can participate.

"I do a site survey and photograph the site with a 35mm camera. I shoot close-ups of window areas, the entryway, and the front doors, ornamental details, and undersurfaces, and get 4-by-6-inch glossy prints. I cover a table with white paper and, working in natural light, make a list of the 'givens'—what's interesting and what's not, the surroundings, the colors of the roof, stone, tile, landing, stained glass, the exposure and orientation.

"Then I give clients a detailed questionnaire with questions like: How do you envision the building? Do you want to make a strong statement?

"Then I develop three to seven schemes showing different color combinations and develop a sample board. I can arrive at a general idea of hues and the overall look of the finished house. I select the number of colors to be used, depending on the number of architectural pieces, accents, etc. But the preliminary color scheme can't be final until the colors are tested on the building itself and seen in light and shadow."

Selecting colors can be intimidating. Working with color on a grand scale, in public, has a visual impact on the whole neighborhood. Tastes and color styles change, along with architectural designs and fashions. Jill gleans the best techniques from the past and combines them with imaginative contemporary solutions, such as exterior stenciling, *trompe l'oeil*, and *faux* finishing.

She feels that four to six colors are the easiest to arrange on a building, especially one with Victorian architecture, which provides many planes for color. A twenty-color scheme may lack dimension and may compete with the building's architecture. A three-color scheme is hard to arrange consistently. Four or more lets you orchestrate the surfaces and doesn't look overdone or busy. She usually finds an aesthetic balance in four different values: a light, a dark, a medium light, and a medium dark.

Jill's rules of color:

1. *Intensity.* Color intensity increases as the volume and scale of color increase. Select grayed and muted hues on large areas. Exterior light amplifies the intensity of color. What may look dull on a paint chip will become very lively on a large expanse.
2. *Balance.* A well-balanced color arrangement will have visual unity. Distribute color evenly over the building, from the top, or hat, to the middle, or belt, to the base, or shoes. A building with a light color base and dark peak may feel top-heavy and ungrounded.
3. *Rhythm.* Keep the same colors touching and interacting for a color juxtaposition that pleases the eye.
4. *Durability.* Select colors that are durable and neutral for major surfaces, and remember that the sun will fade pure bright tones quickly.
5. *Accent colors.* Use strong colors only in small areas so they'll fade gracefully. Jill likes to use accents on undersurfaces, such as soffits, to add an element of surprise and create surface texture.
6. *Skeletal structure.* Use your trim to create a skeletal structure for the building to define and unify the architectural elements.
7. *Interaction.* White drains color from the color it is touching. Black accentuates the color it touches. Gray is a chameleon color; it makes whatever it touches resonate. If gray is touching red, it makes the red appear redder and it takes on a reddish cast itself.
8. *Simplicity.* Just because something has a wood trim around it doesn't mean it has to be accented. Sometimes windows are added after the building was originally finished. So if it's better to play something down, play it down.
9. *Mother Nature.* Certain colors look better on a north face, which receives a cold light. The sun rarely illuminates the structure, so you can color it dark and use more saturated, richer, brighter colors than you can on a south side. This can compensate for the lack of light by creating color glow or radiance. Houses with southern exposures receive the harshest light. They are usually illuminated all day. In this case, lighter value colors are preferable because they resist fading.

On an east face, golden yellow morning light hits the building. This may shift color tones to the yellow side.

On a west face, the warm pink light of the setting sun will affect colors. A neutral taupe can be pink on the west side. "When Mother Nature puts her light system on—watch out."

Jill has discovered that women's eyes see blue-based colors and men's eyes see yellow-based colors, which is why husbands and wives don't always see eye-to-eye on color.

When choosing color, Jill thinks of Frank Lloyd Wright's principle of looking at the site and what would enchance it. She also suggest that you bend your paint chips or fan decks so they touch each other. The critical relationship between colors is their contrast in hue and value. If the contrast is too soft, the planes will flatten out and you will not be able to separate the colors visually.

"The more I learn about color, the better. I started only intuitively; now my choices are more intellectual. Color is a science. For example, I knew that purple fades quickly. Each color vibrates at a specific frequency. Purple fades fast because it vibrates fast. Red vibrates really slowly, so it fades slowly."

When choosing colors, she works scientifically, using the Munsell color box of swatches of tones and hues. The Plochere color box system is not as universally popular, but Jill still uses it for inspiration.

She insists that you must sample colors on the site. Buy a quart of each color and paint the trim next to the body, next to the sash, next to the accent. Sometimes it can take a full day just to swatch every area on a building.

As Jill swatches, she may tint a color by adding white to lighten it, or shade it by adding black to darken it. If two adjacent colors don't harmonize, she mixes some of one color into the other, and vice versa, creating an "essence-of-one-another" relationship.

Then Jill brushes out the selected mixed colors on a color board and writes a specification sheet. One copy is for the client, one for the paint store, one for the records, and one for the contractor. The spec sheet indicates what surfaces should be flat or semigloss. She climbs the scaffold and numbers the building, writing with pencil on the primed building. At this point, the color selection sometimes changes—when she sees how a molding is shaped, for example. This process helps eliminate loose ends. Everything is marked and the painter knows exactly what to do.

Jill enjoys using *faux* finishes for their playful quality and theatricality. Two-story columns of real marble would be too costly, but *faux* marble creates a look of elegance. Some finishes can be too labor intensive or delicate for exteriors. She's enthusiastic about the revival of some crafts, and uses stenciling on exterior designs to heighten people's awareness, as the stencil design creates texture with paint. She's always searching for new ways to ornament a house.

She loves north façades, where she can use any color in the world, especially rich, deep, dark, Oriental colors. She wants to do a Gauguin house in deep russet, plums, teals, golds—jewel-like, saturated colors.

"These buildings are so glorious that it requires a trained eye to allow their beauty to radiate. Harmony and balance are the key. To have harmony, you have to have interaction. With people, you hold hands. With paints, it's colors."

DONI TUNHEIM

"When I was a kid, I had a huge box of Crayolas and I dipped in at will, coloring everything that got in front of me. Today, at the office, I have a large box of paint chips next to my desk, and I dip in it at will, always looking for the next best color. When I'm designing houses, I look for color, not paint."

Doni Tunheim is a vivid, vibrant, sparkling woman, passionate about color. A fourth-generation Californian, Doni was born in 1941 and grew up in the Southern California town of Bakersfield, where there was one Victorian in town. That's the house Doni always wanted. She was always interested in art, illustration, and graphics, and she studied art and graphics at San Jose State.

In college, Doni met Ed Tunheim, a consulting forester. They used to spend Sunday afternoons driving around looking at Victorians, yearning for one of their own. A big neglected Italianate on Green Street in Santa Cruz kept pleading for help. Over the years, they kept driving and kept saving money. Finally, they had saved enough money for a long vacation in Mexico. But in 1964, on their last drive before leaving town, they saw the house they had always wanted for sale.

Actually, what was on sale was the lot. The house was advertised as "condemned," and had to be either repaired or torn down. It was such a poor risk, they couldn't persuade a bank to help with a loan. It was twenty-six years before they got to Mexico.

Doni free-lanced, doing commercial art and graphics, and had two boys, Sam, now nineteen, and Bodi, twenty-two.

In 1966, a friend bought the big Victorian house on the corner. By that time, Doni's Italianate was rust, gray, and blue. Three colors on houses was a new trend. The friend asked Doni about colors. So she picked out gray, white, and blue. And she got paid!

She realized she could be a color designer when a painter asked her for the specific colors she had prescribed for her friend's house. Doni wouldn't tell him because someone else had paid for her for those colors.

Doni feels that painters pick out more colors for houses than anybody else—and that they now usually just pick gray, white, and ice blue. But most of her clients come to her by word of mouth from painters and architects.

Doni Tunheim at home, with color fan decks.

(*Top*). Queen Anne house in Santa Cruz designed by Doni Tunheim.

(*Left*). Doni Tunheim's home in Santa Cruz. (DK)

(*Above*). Doni Tunheim's brightly colored business card.

Tunheim still enjoys doing graphics. One client in Los Banos, inland, flies her in his private plane to oversee not only the exterior of his building, but also the interior and all of the graphics for the company, from the stationery to the logo.

"I like to tell people that they will have their very own color job that no one else will have."

She tries to have her clients agree on colors first, before selecting housepaints. A Tunheim rule: Don't ask everybody in the house to vote on colors; it's too counterproductive.

She does ask her clients if they want a dignified house or a happy house. She goes into their home and tries to find out what kind of people they are, what colors they choose for their clothing and surroundings. Are they shy? Outgoing? She works with them, fanning out paint decks, trying to find their color preferences and prejudices. She also considers the style and size of the house, where it's located, and what's around it.

Then she thinks about it, then she does four sets of colors, putting the chips in a line. She talks about what the colors are, and where they'll go.

"Sometimes I look at a house and it's like a slide show in my head, as the different colors pass in front of my eyes. Then I think and select. I like contrast. Basically, I like to have a balance between lights and darks and I always prefer strong colors. After all, these houses were built for people to be proud of them.

"The cans of paint are like a new box of crayons. I love to see fresh paint go up."

She paints a 2-foot-square flat surface, maybe on the back of the house or garage. Doni recommends buying a quart of each color you're thinking about. "You can't fudge with something as important as your house. We paint a square of body color and then put all the trim colors around it so they touch the body color and each other. Then you can test the colors on your house, taste the combinations."

Sometimes she'll paint all along the back, from top to bottom, from water table to middle layer to top layer including the cornices, so the client can see all the colors together.

"I think houses should be welcoming and look like homes people live in. I'd never use ice blue; it's too cold and depressing. And I don't think you should use gray in California—perhaps you could use it in a hot climate for 'coolth' and serenity. I do think people should use colors that work so that light can bounce off them."

Doni is a firm believer in strong, deep, dark, delicious Victorian colors and disagrees with the belief that they were weak, muddied. She explains that the colors were saturated, therefore much brighter then than they are today.

According to Doni, early paint manufacturers used cadmium and chromium in the yellows, and they were lead based. Today paint has to be nontoxic. She believes that the shine is important on a house, and that oil-based paint should be the bottom layer on old houses. Yet oil-based paints are increasingly difficult to find.

On her own house, Doni used five coats of Chinese red and four coats of her favorite dark oily green semigloss to make the trim bright and lasting. The darker a paint color is, the more transparent it is. The old redwood drank up the paint, necessitating three or more coats.

She wanted a real true yellow, a neglected color, and had to work hard to mix it herself. She used an oil-based primer on the house and it accentuated the dark oily green. One of the trims was "Soaring Jay" white with a bit of green in it. The top coat was a latex semigloss.

She explains that although a flat finish hides imperfections, semigloss gives a rich quality, a depth, and a sparkle. Light bounces off it so it lasts better because it doesn't suck up the light. Doni uses a gloss finish on the doors and frequently uses the same color and finish on the sashes.

Although she likes Victorians best, Doni does color schemes for modern and Craftsman houses. For one ranch-style home, she prescribed rose, navy blue, and cream. A Spanish-style home was done in a peachy pink, a newly favored color on all the Victorians along Ocean View Avenue in Santa Cruz. She does not like the many Neo-Victorian condominiums springing up, since they're never as good as the originals.

After a trip to Colorado, she began thinking about using the Colorado signature, rainbow-colored shingled gables. She's cautious about "getting cute with too much detailing since even a wedding cake can be beyond good taste."

Her most frustrating job was for an inn in the middle of dusty fields in the wine country. After a long drive, Doni found the owner sitting there with two paint chips, one white, one off-white. He asked which one he should use. Doni suggested white, knowing that off-white would look dirty. The inn was painted off-white anyway and, sure enough, it looks dirty.

Not all her color design work is on residental buildings. Doni's favorite job is Santa Cruz's Boardwalk, the only existing beach boardwalk on the West Coast. The huge structure had to be completely rebuilt and restored, since all of the terra cotta trim and plasterwork had been stripped. The huge pillars were reminiscent of the columns in the Minoan Palace of Knossos on Crete, so Doni prescribed custom Tuscan colors: a soft yellow, glowing deep turquoise, rich terra cotta, dark oily green, shining Pompeiian red, grays, and blues. She had to work so fast that she actually penciled in the color design on the walls and the painters followed her the same day. Seeing the yellows, reds, and turquoises from the nearby wharf still makes her happy.

For Doni, a dream client would be someone who believes she can understand him and do the right thing. She would also like to do a Classical Revival or *Beaux Arts* house. And if she ever got the chance, she'd paint San Francisco's City Hall in poppy and gold and green—like California poppies.

"Gray is the beige of the eighties. I try to keep working and looking to see what's new. Right now, everyone's using pastels, the Southwest colors, mauves and peaches. In the future, we may see more creams and whites, perhaps a reaction against the gray.

"I want to paint with a fresh eye, to use new colors. I really like color and want it used. I want to keep using old-fashioned glowing colors." When the people of Santa Cruz see Doni's brilliant tomato-red and turquoise signs (large versions of her business card, seen on page 72), in front of newly bedecked Painted Ladies, they know she's doing just that.

Designers at Play

To offer you creative alternatives that you may be able to use on your house, we asked the color consultants to create schemes for the most popular Victorian house styles: Carpenter Gothic, mansard, Italianate, Queen Anne, and Stick/Eastlake.

All of the houses appear in yet another color scheme in *Painted Ladies* or *Daughters of Painted Ladies*. The Stick/Eastlake house in San Francisco we chose is on the back cover of *Painted Ladies*.

The other five houses are in *Daughters*: the Queen Anne with lion's heads in Buffalo is on page 35, the Carpenter Gothic cottage in Cape May on page 41, the Queen Anne with the seven-sided bay in New Orleans on page 54, the mansard home in Helena, Montana, on page 99, and the Italianate in Coupeville, Washington, on page 103. With the exception of the house in New Orleans, the color schemes in the books were done by the owners.

Something for Everyone

There is something for every taste in these drawings. The designs and colors range from the sedate to the exuberant. Keep in mind that what looks quiet on paper looks brighter on wood.

Most of the colorists did schemes similar to ones that they have already done and that they know will work. A couple of them, however, took this opportunity to use colors and create schemes they would like to use but have not yet had clients who would let them.

The colorists had contrasting reactions to doing the designs. Some found it harder to create schemes without having clients provide their color preferences as a basis for the designs.

None of the colorists knew what the other colorists were doing. For the most part, they also didn't know what houses they were working on. The New Orleans house must have looked familiar to Bob Buckter, because he did the design of the house that appears in *Daughters*. This gives you the chance to see how a colorist approaches a house the second time around. And even though David Irvin did look at the rose-colored Italianate in *Daughters*, he still created a design around whatever-you-do-don't-call-it-pink, because he wanted to do a pink house.

Some readers may be surprised that the most colorful designs are by consultants outside of San Francisco. In the decade since *Painted Ladies* was published, local colorists have muted their palettes into a new range of colors used to create a new generation of Painted Ladies that are celebrated in *Painted Ladies Revisited*.

A Slice of History

Roger Moss and his wife, Gail Caskey Winkler, are the authors of the basic reference guide for painting Victorians in an authentic fashion: *Victorian Exterior Decoration: How to Paint Your Nineteenth-Century American House Historically*.

One basic decision you will have to make is whether you want to paint your house in a historical or in a contemporary style. In *Victorian Exterior Decoration*, Roger and Gail note that you have three choices in deciding how to go about choosing the paint scheme for your home:

1. The scientific approach—you analyze what was originally on the house and reproduce it.
2. The historical approach—the colors and how they are placed are determined by the age and style of your home and how such houses were painted at the time.
3. The boutique approach—you use whatever colors in whatever way pleases you most.

This is a choice that you have to make, but so long as you are guided by good taste and love and respect for your home, you can't go wrong. We feel that since you're going to pay to have your house done, and then live with the results, you should have the right to decide how your home should be painted. But what is essential is to take care of your home, not just to protect your investment but to preserve a small part of America's cultural heritage.

For a historical perspective on how these houses were painted, we asked Roger to describe the colors Victorians used on houses like these. As an example of the fascinating similarities and contrasts that emerge from Roger's analysis, consider the Stick/Eastlake House.

Of the six houses, the Stick/Eastlake is the most richly decorated. Since the architecture creates the opportunities for using color, the designs for this house are the most colorful set of drawings. Yet Roger notes that this house probably would have been painted white to let the play of light and shadow reveal the architecture. This was James Martin's approach to designing the colors, which is why his color scheme is the subtlest of the six. Also worth noting is the intriguing affinity in the designs for this house by Doni Tunheim and David Irvin.

Your Turn

Black-and-white drawings of the houses are

included, starting on page 150. You can photocopy them, enlarge them if you wish, and experiment with your favorite colors.

Enjoying these color schemes is a pleasure worth repeating. You will find unexpected felicities in color and design, surprises that will repay your close attention to detail. Compare these designs and you will find ideas for creating the right color scheme for your home.

JOE ADAMO

"It's harder to do a drawing without the building in front of you. This way, I felt I wasn't going to know how things turned out until it was over. Normally, I use quarts of paint and test on the building itself. I used the Porter Paints palette for the colors. Picking out six combinations of eight colors each—that would be easy. But you wouldn't be getting the love I usually put into a building."

The Carpenter Gothic Cottage

"I went for a dollhouse effect on this cottage. I imagined something my daughter would play with— something delicate, playful, feminine, childlike. Just being in the shadows under the porch makes the bottom story a different color, but I emphasized the difference. The accent on the two railings and the roof line unified the house, tied the whole thing in and pulled it together. If your cornice is very dark or outstanding, and you don't bring it down to other levels of the house, it sort of floats up there. This treatment brings the design together."

The six colors:
1. Pale amethyst, light violet. 3-18-4P
2. Mulberry, darker violet. 3-18-2B
3. Painted Daisy, dark violet-pink. 3-18-5R
4. Light Apricot. 3-23-3P
5. Cowry Pink, a light pinkish peach. 3-23-1R
6. Dark Reseda, medium gray-green, for gutters. 4-30-3P

R. SPOKOWSKI

JOE ADAMO

The Mansard Home

"I knew what I wanted and where on this house, and I'm satisfied with what I see on the rendering. This is like a St. Louis brick house. There's woodwork, brick, and concrete. Different limestone can range in colors from deep red to tan to marbleized old gray. I chose a limestone or sandstone effect, with mottled color on the brick. I really like this and the good bulky colors. This is exactly what I'd have done with a brick house in St. Louis."

The four colors:
1. Moon Mist, pinky tan. 3-27-1P
2. Taupe Mist, pinky gray. 3-27-4P
3. Shadow Rose, a darker grayed pink. 3-21-5P
4. Brick Color: Sahara sand. 3-25-5P

R. SPOKOWSKI

JOE ADAMO

The Italianate

"To me, this looks like a typical San Francisco house, so it needs more colors than other houses. It looks green, red, and brown in the rendering. But there are more colors on the palette I provided. The palette calls for five different colors. If I had been painting this house, I would have changed the colors, darker to lighter, then into greens. In my mind's eye, I saw a better gradation of color."

The six colors:
1. Toast, dark tan. 4-25-2R
2. Etruscan, deep browned red. 4-21-2R
3. Bayberry green. 4-10-2R
4. Asparagus stalk, a medium browned green. 5-9-3T
5. Apricot. 3-22-5R
6. Cinnamon, a lighter, clearer version of the Etruscan Red. 4-21-1T

R SPOKOWSKI

The Stately Queen Anne

"This house reminds me of the houses in Brooklyn, in Flatbush, the mansions I grew up near. They were queenly looking, standing there in dark grays and browns. I imagined this house in a quiet neighborhood, and made it more subdued, sophisticated, dignified. I like the reddish roof tiles and the pink-red accents here. It reminds me of home."

The six colors:

1. Poplar, khaki beige, for the upper body. 4-28-4P
2. Cobblestone gray for the lower body. 4-31-3P
3. Deep mauve, browned. 4-21-4P
4. Shadow Rose, tannish lavender. 3-21-5P
5. Seastone. 4-32-4P
6. Salem Blue, New England blue. 4-15-4P

R. SPOKOWSKI

JOE ADAMO

The Embellished Queen Anne

"This house is lacy, and I found a color I thought fitting for this type of house. I thought it looked better with not much color. This is a big house and I didn't want it to be too overpowering. The lacy effect is good, so I emphasized the vertical and horizontal framing lines. The body color and the lines around the windows and doors are important. I used creamy off-white to give it contrast, to keep it light looking. Even though it's dark, the house is not heavy."

The four colors:
1. Greenstone Gray. 4-30-5P
2. Cumberland Gray. 4-30-4R
3. Melon, a creamy dark tan. 3-4-1P
4. Tile, Red Earth, a rich medium red-brown. 5-21-3T

R. SPOROWSKY

"It was not easy to do these color schemes, because usually I work with many telephoto-lens shots. And, of course, I rarely do this without consulting with the owners and getting input from them. I tried for variety in doing these houses. I wanted to do a yellow house for a change, and a gray-violet one because that's popular now. In all these cases, the color schemes have not been done before. And unless noted otherwise, all the colors are my own invention, what I call BB Color."

The Carpenter Gothic Cottage

"This is a yellow house with accents. Earth tones and yellow were 'out' as house colors for many years and they're just beginning to come back in popularity."
The six colors:
1. Sunshine yellow for the main body.
2. Bone white for the main trim.
3. Burnt sienna, a Sinclair Standard factory-ground color.
4. Dark blue-gray as the facilitator or background color.
5. Brown Owl, a Custom Que color.
6. Norwood Brown, a reddish brown.

R. SPOKOWSKI

The Mansard Home

"I chose salmons and cinnamons for this relatively small house, because the Southwest influence is still popular and salmon is very current. The #3 accent, Catawba, is a dark teal that has been grayed with Mishima. A woman who worked for Benjamin Moore named the color. She thought "grayed teal" would not do—so, since it looked like Lake Michigan in winter, she called it Catawba after a Lake Michigan Indian chief."

The six colors:
1. Salmon, the main body color.
2. Bone white for the main trim.
3. Catawba, grayed teal.
4. Brandywine.
5. Cinnamon.
6. Nut Brown.

R. SPOKOWSKI

The Italianate

"The really popular colors of the eighties are grays, and I picked gray-violets and aubergine for this one, with off-white as the major trim to make the house more lighthearted. The main body color, Golden Gate Bridge 50, was named because I eye-matched it on the day of the bridge's fiftieth anniversary. The aubergine was formulated especially for its durability. The major trim was put on vertically, at the top, middle, and bottom. Then I opted for quiet color on the friezes, the portico, and the bay, so it wouldn't be too busy, too much to believe. I didn't want to go beyond believability and general good taste."

The five colors:

1. Golden Gate Bridge 50, gray-violet, the main body color.
2. Bone white, the main trim.
3. Mishima, a teal–dark green.
4. Brandywine.
5. Aubergine, rich, dark eggplant purple.

R SPOKOWSKI

BOB BUCKTER

The Stately Queen Anne

"In keeping with the dignified weight of the house, I chose a simple, old-fashioned scheme. The colors are eighteenth-century colors I'm especially fond of. The darkest accent, Brackenhouse Slate Gray, is an Old Williamsburg color named for a house in Colonial Williamsburg. And Mississippi Delta, that gray-violet-brown, is what I call a catalyst color. Sometimes you can't even see it, or you're not aware of it, but it pulls all the other colors together. The darker cream main trim gives the house more weight, although anything darker would make it too heavy.

The six colors:
1. Dusty Rose, the main body color.
2. Oyster, the main trim.
3. Ultra Blue Shade, a sturdy navy color, the primary accent.
4. Trianon, a bright Kelly Moore purple.
5. Mississippi Delta, gray violet-brown.
6. Brackenhouse Slate Gray.

R.SPOKOWSKI

The Embellished Queen Anne

"I was aiming for darks and lights on a dark house and ended up with this subtle, sophisticated look in eight colors. The Oyster is darker and creamier than bone, better than bone with a darker body. And even though I used Hunter Green on this house and the Stick/Eastlake, they are from different paint companies, and they are different colors. The turquoise jazzes things up, while the dark gray serves as a catalyst color. The gold leaf gleams in the sun and gives it a special fillip.

The eight colors:
1. Wyandotte Slate, a gray-green teal.
2. Oyster white.
3. Aubergine.
4. Hunter Green.
5. Dark Charcoal Blue.
6. Turquoise.
7. Dark Gray.
8. Gold leaf.

The Stick/Eastlake House

"A century ago, people picked up on the colors in their stained-glass windows when painting their houses. So for this one, I colored the stained-glass window, and then used those colors on the house. I chose dark gray-green for the main theme because olives are really hot now. There aren't too many green houses and we try to stay ahead of color styles and start new trends, to get into new areas. Even though this is the grays decade—as the seventies were an earth tones decade, people don't like or request greens or yellows and can rarely identify gray-violets. And although these colors look relatively dark on paper, remember that when color goes on a building, it's more potent than on any chip or drawing. The bone and careful uses of wines and greens will wake up the grays."

The six colors:
1. Spec Green Dark.
2. Bone white.
3. Ultra Blue Shade, a mix of Ultra Blue and Ultra Black that lasts forever.
4. New London Burgundy.
5. Dark Hunter Green.
6. Dark gray.

R. SPOKOWSKI

DAVID IRVIN

"When we were preparing to color each of these houses, we looked at the photographs in the books, because they showed the details better than the artwork. We named some of the houses as well, to make them more real for us. My assistant, Richard Zingré, worked with me on some of the renderings. We usually provide our clients with hand-colored renderings, since it's easier for them to visualize the finished work that way. [The frontispiece of this book is an example of such a rendering.] Sometimes we offer three or four different color schemes. I don't believe there is one solution for any house. I probably could have used the same color scheme with all the houses. But that wouldn't have been any fun." Unless noted, the colors are from Pratt & Lambert.

The Carpenter Gothic Cottage

"This is our teal scheme in next year's colors. We used two colors of teal and a buff that's so nice that when you paint it, it's like butter. It makes you hungry. The red is bright enough so it pops; it always works, always gets attention. Note the 'wasp-proof ceiling' on the porch."

The eight colors:
1. First floor: Indigo, darkest teal. B706A
2. Second floor: Cruise Blue, medium teal. BG636A
3. Shell coral, clear peach, for window trim and for highlighting recessed scrollwork in the cornice bracket. R0193P
4. Shantung on column and frieze. Y344W
5. River Rouge, accent red. R117A
6. Spanish Blue, dark, clear sea blue, for accent. B769A
7. Winter Sky, pale blue porch ceiling. B721W
8. Base Green.

R. SPOKOWSKI

The Mansard Home

"In *Daughters of Painted Ladies*, this brick house was called the Christmas House, so I had to give it Christmas colors. I like to be true to brick and limestone. We like to decide the house color first. I said to myself, 'This is a red box.' Then we apply new colors in building blocks to the sides of the house, the cornices, the brackets. We also like to change colors at inside corners rather than the outside corner. This is harder on painters and they resist me sometimes, but the clearer result is worth it.

"The lower board is one piece and it should all be same color. The brackets are made like sandwiches. We colored the inside piece one color and the two outer pieces another. The results are a recess of contrasting color on the front of the bracket and the fancy cutouts on the sides being painted so that the color of the inside piece shows through. Red brick is heavy, down to earth, attached to earth, so we had light elements coming out from it to emphasize them."

The nine colors:

1. Cobbler Brown, a dark black-brown, for roof shingles. R125A
2. River Rouge, wine-maroon, for stripes, accents, and window sash. R1117A
3. Fawn Pink, the "p" word for strips and accents. R156P
4. Canyon Orange, for strips and accents. 0212W
5. Tangelo, (medium orange) for strips. 0220M
6. Light Olive, for frieze, soffit, columns, doors. YG525M
7. Shaded Spruce, darkest blue-green, for window frames, steps, keystones, accent panels. BG650A.
8. Hermiston Red, brick color, browny red. R018IA
9. Light Stone, stone tan, for base, window, hoods, stair risers. Y392P
10. Gold leaf accent color, ornamental iron around ridge crest.
11. Shaded Spruce brackets with Canyon Orange relief.
12. Provide River Rouge accent on bracket tear drops.

R. SPOKOWSKI

The Italianate

"I call this one 'Fawn Italianate.' The first version I envisioned was dark red, with peach highlighting the bands and a light bay, but then I changed to a pink base. Pink was the last thing we chose here. We did the buff and peach and chose red as the box color. Then peach was our structural color, with buff as background color. We had to have three colors on the window, each holding a sawn decoration. I always feel that if it's there, we have to highlight it."

The seven colors:

1. Fawn Pink for siding. R156P
2. Evening Sun, medium pink-peach, for columns, corner boards, risers, brackets, recessed panels, horizontal bands, and window trim. 0219P
3. Canyon Orange for soffit, fascia, frieze, bay (base coat), porch ceiling, door panels, and sidelight. 0212W
4. Shadowy Evergreen, darkest grayed green, for bracket side relief, porch brackets, bay column detail. G587A
5. Algerian, brown-toned blood maroon, for door, gutter, recess panel outline, horizontal accent, window heads, and porch post bases. R138R
6. Academy Blue, New England blue, for window sashes, storms, bracket face recesses, and door molding. B7484
7. Spectrum Brown for porch floors and molding between soffit and frieze. R0187A

R SPOKOWSKI

The Stately Queen Anne

"I called this The Turret House, and colored it three shades of blue. The color scheme is like what I used on my own house in Fort Scott. The darker-to-lighter range makes the house look lighter and perhaps taller. The design lifts the house to the sky. Again, we remained true to the materials here. I think leaves should be green and I put in red berries. A lion's mane is always gold, so I used gold leaf."

The eleven colors:

1. Lava for roof slate, porch roof, and gable rooflets. B7996A
2. Algerian for stripes and accents. R138R
3. Deep Jungle, darkest green, for carved foliage, scalloped shingles, stripes, accents. G601A
4. French Vanilla, structural color for window casing, porch spindles, and strips. Y317W
5. Postal Blue, darkest blue, for all blue stripes and blue accents. BU013A
6. Winter Sky, pale blue, for gable backgrounds, third-floor turret siding. B721W
7. Lambert's Blue, second-floor siding only. B741M
8. Ensign, first-floor siding only. B720A
9. Stratum Rock, mud color, for porch floor and stone base and steps. Y356A
10. Shell coral, pearly peach, for lion faces. R0198P
11. Gold leaf for lion manes and highlights in porch gable.

Note: Third-floor turret windows should match second-floor windows.

R SPOKOWSKI

The Embellished Queen Anne

"I named this one Columbine House. I always wanted to do a lavender house, but could never get a homeowner to use it, so this was my chance. I like the way lavender interacts with reds and burgundies. I see B and C working together and C and D working together. Then I tie it all in. I made the roof slate and also used the color for negative spaces that resemble windows, for example, the panels under the bay."

The six colors:

1. Lava, slate roof and all roof sections, scalloped shingles, panels under the turret, and on the bottom point of turret. B796A
2. Cedar Rose, a medium-clear dark pink, for the turret, porch posts and rails, window trim, eave molding, quoins, dentils, and squares in gable. RU095M
3. Botticelli, dark crimson wine, for roof ridges, eaves trim (roof edge), porch spindles, quoin edges, dots on porch posts, sunburst center-balls, filigree background, and dots on the gable squares. RV096GA
4. Columbine, a medium dark grayed lavender, for siding. V084M
5. Shantung for the cornice, quoin background, porch rail circles, sunburst, filigree foreground, and gable background. Y344W
6. Imperial, dark wine grape, for window sashes, eave molding, the edge on "lava" panels, and porch heads. BU034A

R. SPOKOWSKI

The Stick/Eastlake House

"There was so much *stuff* on this house that we had a field day. The main box with quoins looks like masonry, so we chose a masonry color for the structure. We used dark teal for the siding and then wanted to pull the bay out with light background and dark details. There's a light base on the bay. We detailed it up, then darkened in the structural color, so the house thinks it looks like it's being held up. There's so much depth here, it was hard to see how much architectural detail this house really had. If we were really painting this house, I'm sure we would add colors as we discovered more details on the house."

The thirteen colors:

1. Silver Mink, gray-green, on roof shingle. Y399P
2. Algerian Red for stripes and accents and window sash. R138R
3. Victoria Blue on the stripes. B699A
4. Peanut Shell beige on the base rustication and quoins. Y0289P
5. Leafy Bower, dark green, for background and recessed panels. BG671A
6. Shantung background. Y344W
7. Tangelo on columns, accent strips, cornice brackets. 0220M
8. Brick Dust, medium brown-red column accent. R0201A
9. Russet, medium brown, for Corinthian columns and handrails. 0243A
10. Pinecone, medium dark tan, on steps. 0249M
11. Gold leaf for column capitals, bracket accents, detail in the pediment and recess.
12. Provide red accent on relief.
13. Highlight raised areas with red.

R. SPOROWSKI

"People get attached to the drawing when we submit renderings, so I would rather go right to the paint. When I do a drawing, I do a frontal elevation of the house with a sketch showing the pieces, and how they would be colored. Then I color it in black and white to show the different values, and I say which colors would go here and there.

"Since we do a lot of work by mail, I've learned that the only way I can guarantee a job is by specifying the paint. Benjamin Moore has over 1,600 paint colors available all over the country. The chips match the paint. It's solid, long-lasting, based on primary factory-ground colors. This means that the dark color I'm aiming for is the color the company gives me—and the paint will last and not fade. When you use less expensive white- or titanium-based paint, in which the pigment is shot into the mix, then the paint is more prone to separating and fading. And the chips never really match the paint. Sure there may be a difference of up to $20 per gallon, but in the long run, you get what you pay for.

"It's like looking at two denim shirts, one from a name designer and one from the discount store. They may look alike, but you'll find the designer shirt fits better and lasts longer.

"Benjamin Moore colors are really rich, deep, true colors. The wear is excellent and there's a luminosity and vigor I like a lot. I also like latex because the color lasts longer and it doesn't chalk.

"Each hue in the Moore system has eight value steps, so you can really get a nice gradation of color. Paint can look different on the chip than on the house. Something that's pretty on the chip could be screeching on a whole house. I can be accurate with these colors. All the colors here are swatched on the Moore-O-Matic Color System. And remember the code: B for body colors, T for trim colors, P for punch colors, and S for the sash."

The Carpenter Gothic Cottage

"I envisioned this as a Grant Wood–style Midwest farmhouse. I aimed to make it feel light and soft. I played with the detail, making it really subtle, creating a lacy feeling on the sawn-through bargeboard. I use dark colors a lot on the outside of the house as a visual stop. And on the crown molds and gutters, I put a shadow line. It's not a color, it's a deep value, almost a noncolor. You don't see it as a color and may not see it at all. I also use it on doors and shutters. Some days it can look real green, sometimes gray, sometimes sort of blue. The changeability is a treat so you can always get a surprise."

The five colors:
1. B-1—CB41, a sunny sand.
2. P-1—HC158, a dark teal/gray green.
3. T-1—CB 42, a creamy sand.
4. T-2—CB89, a medium sand.
5. T-3—HC86, a dark gray taupe.

R. SPOKOWSKI

The Mansard Home

"On this house I was working with a basic brick color and a brick feeling. It looked like the window had lintels of cut stone, so whether or not this was true, I wanted to give them a feeling of stone, and used stone colors to tie them in with the house. The third punch color would tend to be a bit lighter than it shows on the paper, because that's how the paint really works on a house."

The five browns:
1. B-1—1006, a medium gray-brown taupe.
2. P-1—1166, a dark chocolate brown.
3. P-2—1181, a light milk chocolate.
4. P-3—1252, dark cream.
5. T-1—1079, pale stone.

R. SPOKOWSKI

The Italianate

"I always like to have a theme, a common chord running through the design. This is a harmony of colors; that's not hue, value, or chroma, but the theme. I used light colors on the soffits and porch. And the two trims are the same color, one a darker value of the other. Even though the body has a playful bent, this is a dignified house. Most people do know what they want, they just have a hard time expressing it. I find that most people want a dignified house."

The five colors:
1. B-1—HC137, medium blue-green.
2. P-1—ST63, medium rusty-rosy brown.
3. T-1—GN59, light sand.
4. T-2—GN57, a medium sand.
5. S-1—OW12, a dark sand.

R SPOKOWSKI

The Stately Queen Anne

"This reminded me of houses in Cambridge, Massachusetts. It seems coastal to me, I don't know why, and I wanted to reflect that. I was looking for a crisp feeling. This will look good on a gray morning. I don't usually like cool colors, because I think a house looks and feels better if you use warm colors. But with the blue trim and secondary punch color, this house does have an overall warm feeling.

"I always use a light window sash. I believe that a dark window sash closes the window down. Victorians usually used dark sashes. Victorians seem to have perceived openings as objects, a figurative space. With dark sashes, the space becomes defined, small, and makes the house much darker. Dark sashes give Victorians a musty old feeling. Light sashes open the windows. They're more reflective of how we live, our life today.

"We love having the outside inside. We're open. Light window sashes make the house feel more expansive. I use light overhead surfaces too. When they're dark, the building looms over you. I paint the soffit cornices, the underneath space, the part that's horizontal to the ground, and the inside of the porch ceiling in light colors. This also reflects light into the house better.

The five colors:
1. B-1—1566, medium green-gray blue.
2. B-2—1564, light green-gray blue.
3. T-1—1023, warm, light ivory.
4. P-1—HC 160, intense green-gray blue.
5. P-2—1011, medium taupe.

JAMES MARTIN

The Embellished Queen Anne

"This is a nice scheme for an imposing structure. The brown would cast a rosy hue on the house. The second trim would also have a rosy glow. I know this, because I've used this scheme on a house. I like the red tones underneath all of the tans, and browns, even the periwinkle-lavender trim."

The six colors:

1. B-1—1006, gray taupe.
2. T-1—1010, light taupe.
3. S-1—1009, off-white.
4. P-1—1253, black-brown.
5. P-2—1265, rosy lavender brown.
6. P-3—1426, periwinkle-lavender.

The Stick/Eastlake House

"I wanted to knock as much detail out of this house as I could. It's hard to see what's there. It has so much stuff on it you can hardly get a fix on the building. I wanted to uncomplicate it so that the architecture of the house, the shape and the basic pieces, could show. You don't always have to wave a flag to show the details of the house.

"I used a stone color to make it look like stone, and by using light color, all the detail will shadow. I used a soft off-white to hold the shadow and have the plinths become a color. This will not work, however, if you use a white-white, which will just glare back at you so you can't see anything. Use a light softer color, and it will shadow so the shadow will be soft and pretty, but the stone will show up nicely."

The five colors:
1. B-1—1567, medium blue gray.
2. T-1—1542, stone gray.
3. S-1—1017, ivory.
4. P-1—1014, medium umber.
5. P-2—678, dark bright blue green.

R. SPOKOWSKI

"I want my paint jobs to last, so every one of the color schemes I've done here emphasizes durability. Light colors reflect ultraviolet light and heat. This makes them durable. They outline shape, accentuate detail, and allow light and shadow to play. Dark colors absorb ultraviolet light and heat, making them susceptible to fading. They usually recede, make areas look smaller, but they create drama, weight, and mass. I use dark accents on light buildings, and make sure the body colors are in formulas that will resist weathering and fading."

The Carpenter Gothic Cottage

"This design is a traditional treatment. I saw a farmhouse in a very rural setting. I used traditional green shutters with medium-value taupe in the body, a historical red on the sashes, crispy white trim so the skeletal outline stands on its own, and pale buff to accentuate the sawn work. I kept it very simple. With the traditional dark gray deck I put white risers on the stairs. This keeps them from being too heavy and creates visual action. The screen at the door has to be integrated into an elegant double door, so I colored it the same tone.

"I wanted to focus your attention. The columns were there so you'd know where the door was. The rich green and red reiterates where you go in—and makes you feel welcome."

The seven colors:
1. White trim.
2. Browned slate body.
3. Deep teal shutters.
4. Deep rust sash. 6315N (from Frank W. Dunne, available only in Oakland).
5. Darker cream trim.
6. Dark green-black roof.
7. Dark slate, Mockingbird.

Brick stair treads and brick with red brick edges. Brass doorknob. Black wrought iron on door. Dark green glass in door and transom.

R. SPOKOWSKI

The Mansard Home

"I figured people around the country with brick houses should be inspired. It's a common color challenge: what colors to coordinate with red brick. People do use brick, so I used red brick, with a dark slate mansard roof, traditional red brick, *faux* in the frieze boxes, *faux* marble light gray on sills, and charcoal black-gray *faux* just for the keystones above the windows and window hoods. Brick houses can be interesting. The terrazzo stair material is common, crunched-up stone and marble in cement that lasts forever. The dark door and charcoal black sash are traditional.

"The gable is a large, plain expanse, so I added a shield motif. The terra cotta paint brings brick color to the top of building and stops the eye and finishes the house. This is a classic charcoal-red-gray-and-white combination with *faux* as a playful element."

The eight colors:

1. Brick color, body, Burnt Tile.
2. Classic white trim.
3. Dark charcoal gray sash and door by Fuller.
4. *Faux* marble, Grigio; light gray marble with black.
5. *Faux* marble, Negro; charcoal marble, black vein.
6. Terra cotta, Burnt Tile by Fuller.
7. Traditional slate roof.
8. Gray, white, black speckled terrazzo for the stairway.

Plaster shield in raised plaster plus smaller molding. Masonry foundation. Stone-colored urns.

R. SPOKOWSKI

The Italianate

"This is based on the first house I did in peach, at 219 Douglas in San Francisco. In Mother Nature's light, it looks much peachier. All the colors are Jill-mixed colors eye-matched at Fuller O'Brien.

"I added a wee bit of gold leaf on the columns. Gold leaf is pretty on round or curved surfaces. It bounces and reflects the light. On flat surfaces, it doesn't have the planes to play off of. So I put gold on the sticks on the columnettes. White columnettes around the windows bring the house together like a stoplight shining in the dark. The body on the soffit creates weight and the light brackets provide support. The paint made it all vertical and made the brackets work by holding them up."

The seven colors:

1. Body: Ness Peach—B-44, after Mary Ness, owner of the house.
2. Trim: pink cream, a tauped white, from the Plochere system.
3. Panel mold. B. Swamp—a color from Bradbury & Bradbury wallpaper. I call it Background Swamp, or B. Swamp.
4. Mary Terra Cotta, light pink-brown, for inside box, porch deck, and interior of the boxes.
5. Walden Leaf Sash. Another color from a frieze wallpaper by Bradbury & Bradbury, the leaf from the Iris frieze.
6. B. Swamp mixed with Benjamin Moore Palladian Blue—a blue-green sky under porch.
7. Deck color on tread: a richer darker version of number 4.

Floral-chintz drapes preferred.

R SPOKOWSKI

JILL PILAROSCIA

The Stately Queen Anne

"This house was inspired by a mail-away client in Boston who sent a photo of her house, along with pages from *Daughters*. I did a similar design and the *Boston Globe* wrote about the results.

"There were so many textures on the tower, I wanted to call them out with colors: deep green, paler than deepest blue, and butter, back to base green on top of the tower. I decided to give the house a historical feeling. That's how the building felt architecturally.

"Architecturally, each layer of the house has a different surface texture. Therefore, I wanted to 'transition' color as the surface texture changed. The color is deepest at the base to ground the building. A sky blue porch ceiling. And sitting next to a green wall under a blue sky in my rocker would be a nice thing. I wanted to have a blue to the green side and a green to the blue side. Green felt appropriate for the leaf motif. That's classic associative thinking.

"The yellow advances visually and the coolness of blues and greens recedes nicely. I punctuated the trim by using a light color. There's the traditional cold (medium value) on the deck. Gold leaf adds the glisten. The sashes and casing are both light, because of a complicated window configuration. With both the same color, it's not too busy. It works as one architectural unit. Storm windows, sash, and casements are all the same color.

"I let the variations of the windows play by themselves—the fancy diagonal leaded windows, transomlike windows, double-hung windows, and multiple cross panels. The golden oak door justifies the creaminess of the trim and the gold lions."

The nine colors:

1. For the bottom floor a medium sea green, a traditional green.
2. For the second floor, a medium clear blue-gray.
3. For the top floor and peak area, a light clear blue. With leaf green on the base, and deep blue shingles.
4. Major trim, first floor: eggshell.
5. A darker hue of number 2, which was second-floor body, for the second-floor shingles.
6. Light slate, for cellar and groundwork.
7. For the ring around the lion faces, 24K gold leaf.
8. Dark cream, a regular golden yellow housepaint, for the lion faces.
9. Both roofs: dark medium-value gray-black. A finished wood door in golden oak.

All leaves: Number 1 body, number 6 base. Color in between these two greens.

JILL PILAROSCIA

The Embellished Queen Anne

"I chose these colors from a photo montage in *W* magazine—*Women's Wear Daily.* The olives, with a yellow cast instead of the avocado of the sixties, the plums, and the rust tone are 1988 neutrals. This is a rich scheme and appropriate as a house palette. If this house were in San Francisco, the purple would have to be on the north façade, even if the house were four-sided. Otherwise it wouldn't hold up. I really had fun with this house."

The six colors:

1. Body: a plum based on Martin-Senour interior color 21.
2. Olive: a mix of two olives from the Fuller O'Brien palette.
3. Major trim, light gold.
4. Medium gold.
5. Darkest gold, from Frank W. Dunne.
6. Terra cotta.

R. SPOKOWSKI

JILL PILAROSCIA

The Stick/Eastlake House

"For this one, I used my color scheme for the Henry Street house in San Francisco, all Jill-mixed colors based on the Ameritone system. I pretended the window stained glass was a given, so the colors grew out of the window. This is a complicated building. I wanted to combine cool and warm.

"So this is a study in warm and cool, using both sides of the color wheel. Every color formula has two sides. Purple has red and blue. Every color has many variations. Purple to the red side is red-violet. Purple to the blue side is blue-violet. I like working with this principle, as it gives a scheme complexity and dimension. You can also do it with blue-green/yellow-green combinations. You can see more gradations that way.

"I like to do ribbons of body color to bring the house together. It integrates the bay and the body, even though the planes change. I dislike it when the bay looks glued onto the façade. I want the building woven together. I kept the soffit light and simple because this building is so lofty, I was afraid it would come down on your head emotionally.

"Another trick I have is based on the mathematical formulas of mixing paint. You can mathematically amplify the color. That way you get the same family of colors, but lighter or darker. Tell the paint store: 'I want the formula doubled or halved.' They'll work together with you because they're upping the ante. In the formula, it's like you're mixing a margarita with two ounces of tequila or four ounces, or six ounces. It's still a margarita, just different strengths. For the shingle roof, I blackened the grape color. The door is the body, four times deeper.

"I like using lots of gold leaf on rounded columns and shells. I used a *faux* marble that combined the purple/gold/pink from the sash and columns. The stairs are the trim color and a neutral terrazzo. A Plochere color amplified.

"The door is solid. There's so much happening on the façade, you could pass out. When the entry is only one color, I call it the sorbet. You have a full visual fantasy on the façade, and before people go inside, I like to cool them out a little. Let them take a breath and then enter. Then the interior and exterior don't compete. Here you don't catch your eye on the doorway, so you can keep looking out at the bay and top and everything else. If you paint it out, the eye won't stay there."

The eight colors:

1. Body: Henry Street teal.
2. Medium blue-violet (M3197) for the frame around the box.
3. Trim for the columns: Rich Cream, H 35-1, based on a buff/green/light taupe. A Plochere color developed by a husband-and-wife team in Paris in 1940.
4. Violet maroon for the sash. (HT 155A). A dark ripe burgundy mixed from an Ameritone seven-year-old fan.
5. Lucy Violet, named for the client on Henry Street, for the main portion of bay around windows.
6. Darkened M3179 (close to number 2). Blue–purple grape with red violet, or Lucy Violet, for the main mold.
7. Medium Aqua doors. CM-7
8. Gold leaf.

Neutral terrazzo stairs. Marbleized columns. All shells, gold leaf behind.

R. SPOKOWSKI

"I really enjoyed working on these pictures, enjoyed the total freedom I had to do anything I wanted to do on the houses. It's so rare to have that total control. I liked not having to talk to people, especially people who can't make up their minds.

"Normally, I key colors to the brand of paint the homeowners want to use. And sometimes I make up colors if I can't find them in the paint company's palette. But with these samples, I didn't always cue the colors to a specific paint brand, although many are from the Ameritone palette.

"Since it's hard to divorce things, even houses, from their surroundings, I made up a world around each house to make each more real to me."

The Carpenter Gothic Cottage

"Green is not used enough these days. I love a rich dark oily green and used one with grays here. I also liked the firewheel poppy. I like color to fit the style. Here I wanted to be sure people didn't miss the detail, so used a nice sunny yellow. The light background behind a dark detail works well. Vice versa is also effective."

The six colors used:

1. For the siding: Bark, a dark oily green with brown in it.
2. The major trim: Firewheel, a dark medium orange.
3. Pearly Beige for trim and porch ceiling.
4. Mouse Gray, medium gray, for doors and sash.
5. Blue with lots of black in it for water table, accent, and porch floor.

R. SPOKOWSKI

The Mansard Home

"I feel brick should be brick. But I didn't want the red to be too dominant, so I kept the design light and lively with reds, golds, and creams. I also toyed with the idea of using a lavender as the fourth color instead of the blue-green, and pale gold instead of the bright gold."

The six colors:

1. For the siding: Persimmon.
2. Alligator, dark green, as the door accent.
3. Amberlight, a light cream, for frames, water table trim, and brackets.
4. Kentucky (blue) Grass trim.
5. Bramble, a green-brown, for water table, stairs, sashes, and accents.
6. Brite Gold as major accent.

R.S.POKOWSKI

DONI TUNHEIM

The Italianate

"I always wanted to design a black house. This would be gorgeous. You could only do it in a mild climate, not in intense heat or cold, which expands and contracts the paint too much. I want to bring out the colors of the past, neglected colors, to remind people to use them. This is a warm, friendly house. I live in an Italianate and I love them.

"Working on this picture reminded me that Magic Markers or felt-tip pens really do not work for house renderings. The drawing I marked for the renderer looked gaudy, garish, and fluorescent, not at all like the sample chips—or what I saw in the slide show in my mind."

The eight colors:

1. Midnight, a charcoal black, for the siding.
2. Twilight Blue, a gray lavender-blue, for trim.
3. Burnt red—raspberry or dark wine—for the cornice eaves.
4. Golden harvest, dark gold bronze, for the top of the roof on the porches.
5. Mayan, deep gold-orange pumpkin for trim and boxes.
6. Light yellow gold or eggshell yellow, for the fascia and brackets.
7. Carved ivory, creamy yellow, for the sides of the brackets and porch ceiling.
8. Bolero Rose, a brightener on windows and bay.

R SPOKOWSKI

The Stately Queen Anne

"I pictured this house in a neighborhood with other dignified Queen Annes fighting it out for supremacy. I loved the lions and wanted them to smile. I envisioned a young couple with children and lawn toys all over the yard.

"I wanted to change colors on the stories. This house is so big you have to bring it under control, and the different layers make it smaller. The density of the paint gives new texture and color. Remember that light paint is dense, not see-through. I tried to make the house pink and sunny, to be playful and lively."

The seven colors:

1. Jack-O-Lantern, a shiny gold-orange.
2. Jewel Red, dark magenta for the first story.
3. Baked Apple, medium brown–milk chocolate, for the tower shingles and porch undergable.
4. Pompeiian Wall, a dark dusty rose, for the second story.
5. Sunflower, brightest yellow, for porch ceiling and dentils.
6. Sandrift, a pale pink cream, for the columns and structure trim.
7. Umber Brown for door and liners.

R. SPOKOWSKI

The Embellished Queen Anne

"I tried to downplay this house. Of the six architectural examples, this is my least favorite house because it's so richly decorated. The tower is such a powerful element, I didn't want it to be the only thing you saw. I tied it down to the ground with the gray.

"Never use stark white. Always put a bit of cream or pink in it. Refrigerator white glares, since it reflects 100 percent of the sun's rays. A dark color such as navy or black reflects only 7 percent. So I try to put high-fade colors where they won't fade so fast, such as under eaves. Dark blue fades faster than any other color. It lasts two or three years, tops, but will last longer if you tint your primer too."

The nine colors:

1. A dark green-gray for the structural trim.
2. Nugget, a medium gold–dark tan body color, for the third story.
3. Sentry blue, a medium turquoise or light teal, for the body color on the second story.
4. Oak, a dark tan body color for the first story.
5. Dill, dark green, for windows, trim, dentils, porch, and steps.
6. Pierre, an aggressive teal, for structure and bay trim.
7. Shadoblue.
8. Pale cream for lacework.
9. Gold leaf on the finials.

The Stick/Eastlake House

"It's hard to divorce things from your surroundings. I pictured San Francisco on a cold, foggy day and wanted something warm. I also thought about the city, the buildings next door. This is my statement against people using gray in a gray climate. I wanted to re-introduce brown, a really rich brown, a Hershey bar brown, next to bittersweet, another edible color. Usually, I only use five to seven colors. Here, the architecture is so complex, I had to use eight."

The eight colors:

1. California poppy for accent.
2. Bittersweet, an edible color, for siding or body.
3. Charred oak, dark chocolate brown, for the water table.
4. Ultra Gold, Empire gold, for accent.
5. Blue Fog, dark teal, for accent, porch, and steps.
6. Marsh brown, khaki, for frames.
7. Deep Cavern, darkest teal, for doors and sash.
8. Cream accent for the major trim and shutters.

R. SPOROWSKI

A Historical Perspective

To provide you with a historically accurate alternative to the contemporary approaches of the six colorists, we asked Roger W. Moss to suggest what the original color designs for these houses might have been like.

Robert W. Moss is America's leading authority on Victorian architecture. He is the director of The Athenaeum in Philadelphia, a research library specializing in nineteenth-century history. He teaches in the Historic Preservation Program at the University of Pennsylvania, and lectures and writes extensively on architecture and decorative arts.

To learn more about historically accurate color choice and placement, read *Victorian Exterior Decoration: How to Paint Your Nineteenth-Century Home Historically* by Roger and his wife, Gail Caskey Winkler. Their book is essential reading if you're planning to paint your Victorian in an authentic fashion. But regardless of what color you paint your house, you will find the book a helpful companion to this volume.

You will also enjoy their other joint effort, *Victorian Interior Decoration: American Interiors 1830–1900*; Moss's *Lighting for Historic Buildings: A Guide to Selecting Reproductions*; and *Floor Coverings for Historic Buildings: A Guide to Selecting Reproductions* by Helene von Rosenstiel and Gail Caskey Winkler.

The Carpenter Gothic

"This handsome vernacular cottage owes much of its character to the gothicizing details associated with Andrew Jackson Downing's books of the 1840s and 1850s, but like the Italianate style—which also influences the design—the Gothic remained popular in rural areas well into the century. Downing had strong views on how such houses should be painted. He specifically suggested grays, drab, and fawn (yellowish browns) as "pleasing and harmonious in any situation in the country." The modern owner wishing a historical scheme might adopt light, medium, and dark gray stone colors (such as Sherwin-Williams Oyster Gray, Georgian Gray, and Gray Flannel) or light, medium, and dark drab (Sherwin-Williams Raw Linen, Buckskin Tan, and Loam) or fawn (Sherwin-Williams Green Gold) trimmed with straw (Sherwin-Williams Corn Stalk) or buff (Sherwin-Williams Wax). There is a dangerous temptation to introduce too many colors on such a house. Instead, reversing body and trim colors back and forth in the frieze panels, recesses of cornice brackets, and porch brackets creates a lively façade."

The Mansard Home

"As a general rule, unpainted masonry houses (brick, stone, stucco) were more conservatively painted than clapboard structures of the same age and style. A single trim color, usually simulating brownstone, sandstone, or limestone, would be applied to all wooden trim such as cornices, window frames, and sash, as well as the porch. The object was to make the wooden trim elements appear to have been cut from stone. Sand would sometimes be blown onto the wet paint to heighten the effect. This approach allows for little picking out of details, since stone trim would probably be a single color.

"Such houses often provide color guidance to their owners. If there are genuine stone details (windowsills, lintels, water tables, for example) the color of this stone can be simulated in painting the trim. The overall uniformity thus achieved can be stately and elegant. Roof cresting such as that shown here was usually painted a bronze green in the nineteenth century, colors such as Sherwin-Williams Valley Green, Glidden Town House, or Devoe Ground Pine. This color is neutral and goes well with virtually any stone color that might be selected for the trim."

The Italianate

"Italianate was the most popular American residential style of the mid-nineteenth century. It was first introduced to the East from Scotland and England in 1830s, widely adopted in the Middle West during the decades prior to the Civil War, and continued to spread into the West to the end of the century. Pre–Civil War examples of such bracketed houses are usually painted in two major colors, with earth tones or stone colors predominating. Rather than introduce several colors on the body and trim, one body color and one trim color are selected—for example, a light slate body color for the clapboards and a dark or medium slate trim color for use on cornices, porch, corner boards, window, and door frames. The body color would then be used to highlight the frieze panels of the cornice and the window bay panels and the porch brackets. Sash and porch post chamfers might be reddish brown.

Historical practice usually dictates that the distinctive brackets of the Italianate cornices would be painted in the trim color to match the frieze and soffit of the cornice. They are visually part of the structural system of the roof, and to paint them a different color shows that the painter doesn't understand how the house is put together. Whatever colors are selected, brackets should not float free of the cornice."

The Stately Queen Anne

"The Queen Anne style provides more opportunity for multicolor use: three body colors and a major trim color offset by a dark sash—deep red, green, or even black. This late example, however, has strong Georgian elements on the porch, cornice, and the wonderful carving of the tympanum on the porch and attic. Historical practice favors painting these carvings a single color and quite often a rich terra cotta or, if the desired effect is aged carved English oak, a rich brown might have been used. The owner of this house also has the option to adopt the complex Queen Anne color schemes, or the more (for the time) avant-garde Colonial Revival color, which might call for a yellow body and white trim. By the 1890s a reaction against deep, rich, complex Queen Anne color schemes had set in; as a consequence the simple, light scheme associated with Neoclassical and Colonial architecture returned."

The Embellished Queen Anne

"This house lends itself by style and date to the complex schemes favored by modern colorists, with several colors used to bring out the carved elements and different surface textures. In the nineteenth century, such practice appears commonly on the more exotic Queen Anne houses that were popular in the 1880s and 1890s. Nonetheless, it would be perfectly appropriate from an historical perspective to select a modest scheme and reverse the colors to highlight the changing textures and carved details. For example, the original owner might have selected two shades of olive trimmed with Indian red sash."

The Stick/Eastlake House

"Historically, such late San Francisco houses were probably painted white following the influence of the Columbian Exposition of 1893, turning perhaps to pastels in the early years of the twentieth century. Depending on form and shadow rather than color for their visual impact, such houses must have looked as though chiseled from a block of Carrara marble or carved from Ivory Soap. By the late nineteenth century, gray or gray-and-white schemes were popular. However, we know from the complaints voiced in periodicals of the times that "gaudy coats of brown and yellow, cream and maroon, gray, yellow, pink, red, or olive" joined with some hue in violent contrast were being used by some owners. Such "bizarre" effects seem not to have been common except in seaside communities."

Your Turn

R. SPOKOWSKI

R. SPOKOWSKI

R SPOKOWSKI

R. SPOKOWSKI

R. SPOKOWSKI

154

R. SPOKOWSKI

A Pictorial Glossary

This Pictorial Glossary of architectural terms is a reproduction of the Pictorial Glossary that appears in *Victorian Exterior Decoration: How to Paint Your Nineteenth-Century American House Historically* (New York: Henry Holt & Co., 1987) by Roger W. Moss and Gail Caskey Winkler. The glossary is based on an original document in the collections of The Athenaeum of Philadelphia.

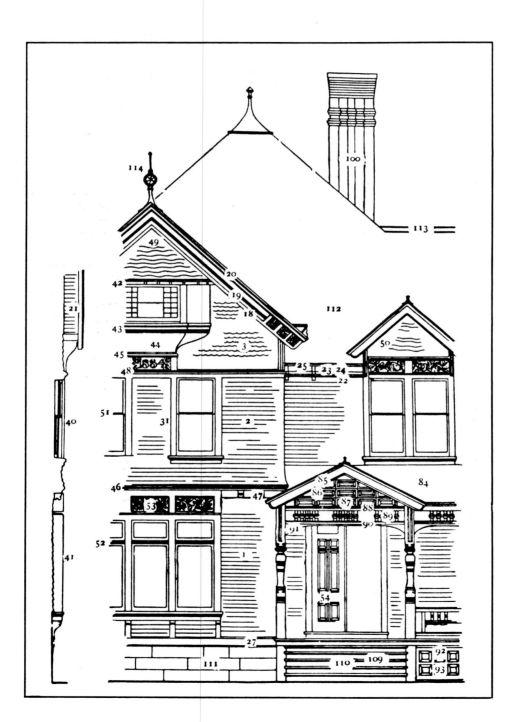

1.–3. Body
1. First story
2. Second story
3. Attic

4.–25. Cornice
4. Edge of crown mold
5. Crown
6. Fascia
7. Bed mold
8. Dentals
9. Frieze
10. Panel mold
11. Panel
12. Architrave
13. Sunken face of sandwich bracket
14. Raised face of sandwich bracket
15. Bracket panel
16. Bracket margin
17. Soffit
18.–20. Bargeboard
21. Ceiling under eaves
22. Foot pieces
23. Gutter face
24. Gutter brackets
25. Gutter cap

26. Corner Board

27.–30. Water Table
28. Slope
29. Edge
30. Face

31.–45. Window Frame or Casing
32. Face
33. Cap fillet
34. Cap mold
35. Cap panel
36. Keystone
37. Chamfer
38. Sill

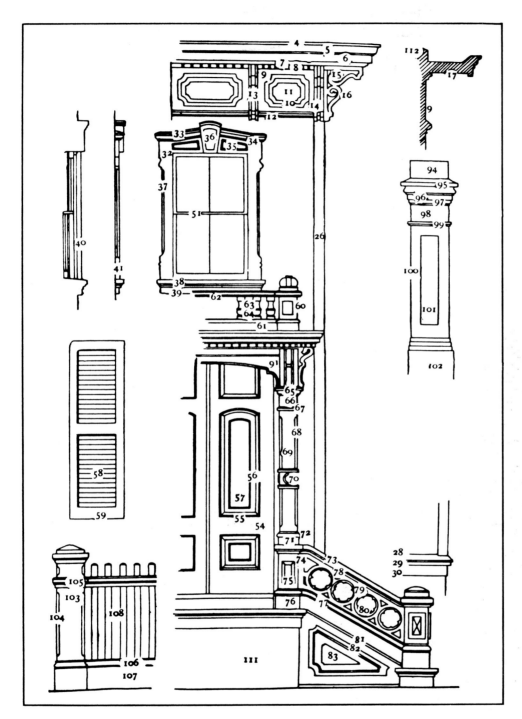

39. Apron
40. Reveal
41. Edge
42. Attic window cornice
43. Attic window sill mold
44. Attic window cove
45. Attic window base mold
46. **Belt Course**
47. **Beam Ends**
48. **Attic Belt Course**
49.–50. **Tympanum**
51. **Window Sash**
52. **Window Transom**
53. **Cut Work**
54.–57. **Doors**
54. Stiles and rails
55. Mold
56. Receding part of panel
57. Projecting part of panel
58.–59. **Shutters (Blinds)**
58. Louvers (slats)
59. Frame
60.–93. **Porch**
60. Balustrade post
61. Balustrade base
62. Balustrade rail
63. Receding part of baluster
64. Projecting part of baluster
65. Abacus
66. Capital
67. Neck mold
68. Chamfer
69. Shaft
70. Rosette
71. Plinth
72. Plinth mold
73. Rail
74. Dado
75. Dado panel
76. Base

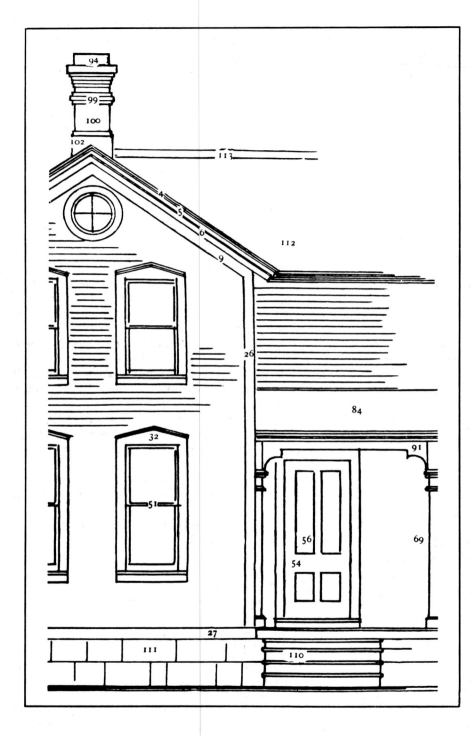

77. Base mold
78. Ornamental rail
79. Ornamental panel
80. Ornamental chamfer
81. Bead below steps
82. Panel mold below steps
83. Panel below steps
84. Roof
85. Face rafter (bargeboard)
86. Gable rail
87. Gable panels
88. Plate
89. Cornice balusters
90. Cornice rail
91. Cornice bracket
92. Rails below
93. Panels below
94.–102. Chimney
94. Top of cap
95. Crown mold of cap
96. Fascia of cap
97. Bed mold of cap
98. Frieze of cap
99. Architrave
100. Shaft
101. Panels
102. Base
103.–108. Fence
103. Post
104. Post chamfer
105. Upper rail
106. Lower rail
107. Base
108. Pickets (balusters)
109.–110. Steps
109. Tread mold
110. Riser
111. Foundation
112.–114. Roof
113. Ridge roll or cresting
114. Iron finials (also common
location for acroterion)

Sample Contractor's Document

Gustavo Caldavelli's Cal Crew of San Francisco provides a detailed plan of work and supplies for each job. For a small two-story job, in which polychrome would be used only on the façade, a fifteen-page document was delivered. In language the layman can understand—and be sure you understand everything before agreeing—the document describes the work planned. This would include the sealing, painting, and finishing of exterior exposed items and surfaces.

Surface preparation, primers, and coats of paint are specified, along with shop-priming and surface treatment.

The *areas* include all exterior visible surfaces, the two west-facing light wells with the adjacent property line wall, soffits, trim, siding, exposed metal surfaces, cement surfaces such as the main stairwell, driveway retaining wall, and miscellaneous areas, window trim and sash, doors and garage door, rear stair steps, and deck.

Color arrangements are spelled out: The exterior will have a base color with door and window trims, trim color, and one or two minor accent colors on the front of the house, the north face. One color is used on the sides and back, the south, east and west elevations.

Field painting of exposed bases and covered pipes, ducts, and ironwork is spelled out.

The definition of *paint* means all coating systems, including primers, emulsions, enamels, stains, sealers, fillers, and other applied materials.

The surfaces to be painted: prefinished items and concealed surfaces are listed.

Also listed is what is not required, such as walls in inaccessible areas, foundation spaces, and finished metal surfaces and operating parts.

Quality assurance is guaranteed, provided that primers and other undercoat paint is produced by the same manufacturer as the finish coats, and only thinners approved by the paint manufacturers, with their recommendations, are used.

Manufacturers are listed.

Materials by name, color, and lead content are listed.

Samples of colors to be used on the house, with sheens, colors, and textures, are listed.

Delivery and storage are accounted for.

Job conditions are covered, including the temperatures to paint in and the humidities. For example, you shouldn't paint latex when it's under 50 degrees or over 90, and if it is over 70, the painters should paint in the shade, not in bright sun. Also, over 85 percent humidity is not recommended.

Execution, including an inspection of the areas and listing of conditions before, during, and after, is specified.

Surface preparation—cleaning, barrier coats, removal of hardware, cleaning of different metals (ferrous and galvanized), cement, and wood—is described.

Materials for preparation are listed.

Application—where, when, how, the schedule of each item, the time between coats, minimum thickness on and around mechanical and electrical items—is specified.

Prime coats are detailed.

Special finishes to be applied, such as stipple finish, transparent finish, or opaque finishes are spelled out.

Cloudiness, spotting, holidays, laps, brush marks, runs, sags, ropiness, or other surface imperfections will not be acceptable.

The complete work is defined.

Field quality control, the right of the owner to check, to stop and test services, is spelled out.

Cleanup and protection are described as the daily removal of rubbish, cans, and rags, and the cleaning of windows, glass, and other spattered surfaces.

The contractor agrees to protection of other people while the crew is working and promises to correct any damage, clean up, and repaint in certain circumstances.

The contractor will provide Wet Paint signs and remove temporary protective wrappings after the job is done.

Paint for each surface, with the correct name and number on, is specified:

concrete and stucco
general painted wood
painted wood trim
painted plywood (ceiling soffits)
prime coat
first and second finish coat
stained wood
ferrous metal
zinc-coated metal
wood stairs and deck

The conclusion incorporates any special considerations either the contractor or the homeowner desires.

Before You Dip Your Brush

This book was written to encourage homeowners to turn their Victorians into works of art. We have tried to make it as helpful as possible, and experts in the field have reviewed it.

Nonetheless, for a volume like this to encompass all of the potential problems homeowners around the country might encounter and to solve them is impossible. We cannot guarantee that the instructions in this book, however carefully devised, will work for you and your house.

To have the best chance of obtaining the best possible paint job on your house, choose one of these alternatives:

1. Find the finest professionals available and encourage them to use the finest materials they can and do whatever is necessary to produce the desired result.

2. *If you decide to paint your house yourself:*

—Read whatever books, magazines, and manufacturer's brochures you can find on the subject.

—Get the advice of other homeowners, suppliers, and professionals in the field.

—Study your home carefully, both to understand what restoration it needs and to develop a sense of what colors and placement will best do the architecture justice and make you happy and proud every time you see it.

—*Prep your house thoroughly before painting it.*

—*Economize with the best. Use top-quality supplies.*

—*Read the labels on all products before using them.*

—*Always follow all safety precautions.*

—*Try several different color schemes to find the one that pleases you most.*

—*Take your time swatching the house and seeing how the colors look in different lights.*

—*Accept the reality that no matter what colors you choose, some people won't like it. Use your common sense and trust your instincts.*

—*Paint your house as a labor of love and with respect for the architecture.*

—*Revel in the chaos!*

Resources

Color Specialists

Joseph Adamo
57 Bradford
San Francisco, CA 94110
415-821-3372

Bob Buckter
Color Consultants
3877 20th Street
San Francisco, CA 94114
415-922-7444

David Irvin, AIA
Irvin Associates
22½ North Main
Fort Scott, KS 66701
316-223-2564

James Martin
The Color People
1546 Williams Street, Suite 201
Denver, CO 80218
303-388-8686

Robert Dufort
Magic Brush, Inc.
1500-B Davidson Avenue
San Francisco, CA 94124
415-641-8622

Roger W. Moss, Director
The Athenaeum of Philadelphia
219 South Sixth Street
Philadelphia, PA 19106
215-925-2688

Jill Pilaroscia
Architectural Colour
220 Eureka Street
San Francisco, CA 94114
415-861-8086

Doni Tunheim
Exterior Interior Building Colors
123 Green Street
Santa Cruz, CA 95060
408-426-6415

Organizations

Association for Preservation
  Technology
P.O. Box 2487, Station D
Ottawa, Ontario
Canada K1P 5W6

The Athenaeum of Philadelphia
219 South Sixth Street
Philadelphia, PA 19106
215-925-2688
Informational pamphlets, library

National Paint & Coatings
  Association
1500 Rhode Island Ave., N.W.
Washington, D.C. 20005
202-462-6272
Information and how-to brochures

National Trust for Historic
  Preservation
1785 Massachusetts Avenue, N.W.
Washington, D.C. 20036
202-673-4000

New York Landmarks Conservancy
Technical Preservation Services
  Center
330 West Forty-Second Street
New York, NY 10036
212-995-5260

**Paint Companies with Traditional
  Palettes**

Color charts and cards available on
  request.

Allentown Paint Manufacturing Co.
P.O. Box 597
Allentown, PA 18105
215-433-4273
Breining's Ready-Mixed oil paints

Ameritone Paint
P.O. Box 190
Long Beach, CA 90801
213-639-6791
Color Key Program

Benjamin Moore & Co.
52 Chestnut Ridge Road
Montvale, NJ 07645
201-573-9600
Historical Color collections

Devoe & Raynolds Company
4000 Dupont Circle
Louisville, KY 40207
502-897-9861
Traditions palette, from 1885 Devoe
  paint catalogue, and Color Key
  Program

Frank W. Dunne Co.
1007 41st Street
Oakland, CA 94608
415-652-1200

Finnaren & Haley, Inc.
2320 Haverford Road
Ardmore, PA 19003
215-649-5000
Colonial colors

Fuller O'Brien Paints
P.O. Box 864
Brunswick, GA 31520
912-265-7650
Victorian and Heritage colors

Martin-Senour Co.
1370 Ontario Avenue, N.W.
Cleveland, OH 44113
800-446-9240
Williamsburg Paint Colors

Muralo Co.
148 East 5th Street
Bayonne, NJ 07002
201-437-0770
Georgetown Colors in 100 percent
  linseed oil;
also calcimine paint

The Old-Fashioned Milk Paint Co.
P.O. Box 222H
Groton, MA 01450
617-448-6336

Pittsburgh Paints
One PPG Place
Pittsburgh, PA 15272
412-434-3131

Porter Paints
1212 Pierce Avenue
St. Louis, MO 63110
314-645-0500

Pratt & Lambert
75 Tonawanda Street
Buffalo, NY 14207
716-873-6000
Early American colors

Sherwin-Williams Company
101 Prospect Avenue
Cleveland, OH 44115
"The Century of Color," Heritage
    Colors
216-566-2332

Stulb Paint & Chemical Co.
P.O. Box 297
Norristown, PA 19404
215-272-6660
Old Sturbridge and Old Village Paint
    Colours

Suppliers: A Selected List

AA Abbingdon Affiliates, Inc.
2149 Utica Avenue
Brooklyn, NY 11234
718-258-8333
Tin ceilings, cornices, and moldings

Abatron, Inc.
141 Center Drive
Gilberts, IL 60136
312-426-2200
LiquidWood and WoodEpoxy

Accurate Metal Weatherstrip Co.
724 South Fulton Avenue
Mt. Vernon, NY 10550
914-668-6042

Advanced Materials, Inc.
Classic Lamp Posts
454–2 Main Street
P.O. Box 917
Deep River, CT 06417
203-526-9755
Restoration and coating products,
wood and metal repair

American Products, Inc.
820 Pearl Street
Racine, WI 53403
800-732-0609
Staircases

Anthony Wood Products, Inc.
113 Industrial Loop
P.O. Box 1081
Hillsboro, TX 76645
817-582-7225
Gingerbread

Antiquaria
60 Dartmouth Street
Springfield, MA 01109
617-862-9073
Victorian furnishings

Architecture in Glass, Inc.
P.O. Box 167
Rowayton, CT 06853
203-853-9983
Conservatories and greenhouses

Art Directions
6120 Delmare Boulevard
St. Louis, MO 6311
314-863-1895
Architectural woodwork and
    glasswork

Artistic License
1925 'A' Fillmore Street
San Francisco, CA 94115
415-922-2854
An affiliation of craftsmen and
    consultants

Aurora Lamp Works
597 East Street
New Haven, CT 06511
203-787-1535

Ball & Ball
463 West Lincoln Highway
Exton, PA 19341
215-363-7330
FAX: 215-363-7639
Hardware and repair

Bay City Paint Co.
2279 Market Street
San Francisco, CA 94114
415-431-4914
Specialty paints, brushes, and
    supplies

Beaver Tool & Supply
P.O. Box 8047
Green Bay, WI 54308
414-436-6300

Besco Plumbing
729 Atlantic Avenue
Boston, MA 02111
617-423-4235

Bradbury & Bradbury
Handprinted Victorian Wallpapers
Box 155
Benicia, CA 94510
707-746-1900

Brasslight
P.O. Box 695
Nyack, NY 10960
914-353-0567

J. R. Burrows & Co.
Victorian Merchant Window
    Coverings
P.O. Box 418 Cathedral Station
Boston, MA 02128
617-451-1982

Chadsworth, Inc.
P.O. Box 53268
Atlanta, GA 30355
404-876-5410
Columns, capitals, bases,
and plinths

Cherry Creek Enterprises
937 Santa Fe Drive
Denver, CO 80204
303-892-1819
Glass fabrications

Chelsea Decorative Metal Co.
9603 Moonlight
Houston, TX 77096
713-721-9200

Christy Cizek
FAUX
264 Manor Drive
Mill Valley, CA 94941
415-383-8113

Classic Architectural Supplies
5302 Junius
Dallas, TX 75214
214-827-5111

Crawford's Old House Store
550 Elizabeth Street
Waukesha, WI 53186
414-542-0685
Victorian hardware

Wyman Chin
Creative Paint & Wallpaper Co.
999 Geary Street
San Francisco, CA 94109
415-441-8850

Cumberland Woodcraft Company,
  Inc.
P.O. Drawer 609
Carlisle, PA 17013
717-243-0063; 800-367-1884
FAX: 717-243-6502
Millwork and fixtures

Custom Ironworks, Inc.
P.O. Box 99
Union, KY 41091
606-384-4486
Iron fencing and gates

Diedrich Chemicals
7373 South Sixth Street
Oak Creek, WI 53154
414-764-0058
Peel-Away and chemical strippers

E & B Marine Supply
980 Gladys Court
P.O. Box 747
Edison, NJ 08818
201-287-3900
Wood epoxies

Erie Landmark Co.
90 West Montgomery Avenue,
  Suite 211
Rockville, MD 20850
301-460-7575
Custom-made building markers

Felber Studios, Inc.
P.O. Box 551
110 Ardmore Avenue
Ardmore, PA 19003–0551
215-642-4710
Ornamental plaster products

Larry W. Garnett & Associates, Inc.,
Building Designers
4710 Vista Road
Pasadena, TX 77505
713-487-0427
Victorian and farmhouse portfolio

Grand Era Reproductions
P.O. Box 1026
Lapeer, MI 48446
313-664-1756
Storm and screen doors

Great America Salvage
34 Cooper Street
New York, NY 10003
212-505-0077
Architectural salvage

Great Lakes Concrete Products
Box 157
Menomonee Falls, WI 53051
414-251-3010

Hamilton Enterprises
2908 Cherry Lane
Northbrook, IL 60062
312-272-0411
Paint scrapers

Heritage Mantels
P.O. Box 671
Southport, CT 06490
203-335-0552

Historical Replications, Inc.
P.O. Box 13529
Jackson, MS 39236
800-426-5628
Floor plans

Home Planners, Inc.
23761 Research Drive
Farmington Hills, MI 48204
313-477-1850
Plan books

Hy-C Company, Inc.
2107 North 14th
St. Louis, MO 63106
314-241-1214
Chimney tops

Interior & Exterior Designs
P.O. Box 2825
Crystal River, FL 32629
904-563-0674
Victorian gingerbread trim patterns

JMR Products
115 Main Street
St. Helena, CA 94574
707-963-7377
Patterned screen doors

LaHaye Bronze, Inc.
1346 Railroad Street
Corona, CA 91720
714-734-1371
Crafts, ornamental metalwork

Langnickel Brushes
229 West Twenty-eighth Street
New York, NY 10001
212-563-9440

The Library
P.O. Box 13529
Jackson, MS 39236
800-426-5638
Architectural embellishments
Books on Victorian architecture

Little/Raidl Art Glass
49 Hartford
San Francisco, CA 94114
415-552-3557

London Lace
167 Newbury Street, Second floor
Boston, MA 02116
617-267-3506

Mad River Woodworks
P.O. Box 163
1355 Guintoli Lane
Arcata, CA 95521
707-826-0629
Gingerbread

Marvin Windows
8043 24th Avenue South
Minneapolis, MN 55420
800-346-5128
Victorian window frames

Matthew Mosca
2513 Queen Anne Boulevard
Baltimore, MD 21216
301-966-5325
Historic paint specialist

MRA Associates
79 Bridge Street
Brooklyn, NY 11201
718-643-0990
Polymer moldings

M. J. Mullane Co.
P.O. Box 108
Hudson, MA 01749
617-568-0597
Snow guards

Munsell Color Notation System
2441 North Calvert Street
Baltimore, MD 21218
301-243-2171
Color charts and information

The New Victorians, Inc.
P.O. Box 32505
Phoenix, AZ 85064
602-956-0755
"Victoriana" plans

Nixalite of America
1025 16th Avenue
P.O. Box 727
East Moline, IL 61244
309-755-8771
Architectural bird control

W. F. Norman Corp.
P.O. Box 323
Nevada, MO 64772-0323
800-641-4038
Architectural sheet metal
ornaments, ceilings

Old Jefferson Tile Co.
P.O. Box 494
Jefferson, TX 75657
214-665-2221

Old World Moulding & Finishing,
 Inc.
115 Allen Boulevard
Farmingdale, NY 11735
516-293-1789

Olde Theatre Architectural
 Salvage Co.
2045 Broadway
Kansas City, MO 64108
816-283-3740

Pagliacco Turning & Milling
P.O. Box 225
Woodacre, CA 94973-0225
415-488-4333
Gingerbread

Park Place
2251 Wisconsin Avenue, N.W.
Washington D.C. 20007
202-342-6294
Victorian exterior trimmings
in wood, glass, and stone

Pasternak's Emporium
2515 Morse Street
Houston, TX 77019
713-528-3808
Victorian gingerbread trim
and wood products

Princeton Plans Press
P.O. Box 622
Princeton, NJ 08540
609-924-9655
Victorian collection

Raleigh, Inc.
1921 Genoa Road
Belvedere, IL 61008
815-544-4141
Roof restoration

Remodelers & Renovators
1920 North Liberty Street
Boise, ID 83704
208-323-1809
Building and decorating products

Renovation Source, Inc.
3512 North Southport Avenue
Chicago, IL 60657
312-327-1250
Architectural trim and old house
 products

Restoration Treasure
Box 724
Cooperstown, NY 13326
315-858-0315
Architectural salvage

Restoration Works, Inc.
P.O. Box 486
Buffalo, NY 14205
716-856-8000
Hardware and fixtures

Renovators' Supply, Inc.
4371 Renovator's Old Mill
P.O. Box 61
Millers Falls, MA 01349
413-659-2211
Oak, porcelain, iron, brass
 accessories

Riverton Corp.
Riverton, VA 22651
800-336-2490
Technical assistance with masonry

Roy Electric Company, Inc.
1054 Coney Island Avenue
Brooklyn, NY 11230
718-339-6311
Electrical supplies

Salvage One
1524 South Sangamon Street
Chicago, IL 60608
312-733-0098
Found treasures

San Francisco Victoriana
2245 Palou Avenue
San Francisco, CA 94124
415-648-0313
Moldings, columns, ornaments,
and wall coverings

A. F. Schwerd Manufacturing Co.
3215 McClure Avenue
Pittsburgh, PA 15212
412-766-6322
Wood columns, cast-aluminum bases

Sepp Leaf Products, Inc.
Suite 1312
381 Park Avenue South
New York, NY 10016
212-683-2840/1
FAX: 212-725-0308
Gold leaf and gilding products

Shades of the Past
Box 502
Corte Madera, CA 94925
415-459-6999
Window shades and curtains

Shuttercraft
282 Stepstone Hill Road
Guilford, CT 06437
203-453-1973

Silverton Victorian Millworks
P.O. Box 2987
Durango, CO 81302
303-259-5915
Gingerbread to order

The Stulb Company
618 West Washington Street
Norristown, PA 19404
215-272-6660

Steptoe & Wife Antiques, Ltd.
Cast Iron
322 Geary Avenue
Toronto, Ontario
Canada M6H 2C7
416-530-4200

Steven F. Stevens
1380 Bush Street
San Francisco, CA 94109
415-885-5236
Stained glass

John Stort & Sons, Inc.
210 Vine Street
Philadelphia, PA 19106
215-627-3855
Hand tools

Sun Designs
P.O. Box 206
Delafield, WI 53018
414-567-4255
Books and plans

United House Wrecking
535 Hope Street
Stamford, CT 06906
203-348-5371
Architectural salvage

Van Dyke's Restorers
Woonsocket, SD 57385
800-843-3320
Gingerbread, brass hardware

Vermont Structural Slate Company,
  Inc.
Fairhaven, Vermont 05743
800-343-1900

Victorian House
128 Longwood Street
Rockford, IL 61107
815-963-3351
Restoration supplies

Victorian Interior Restoration
2321 Sidney Street
P.O. Box 42311
Pillsbury, PA 15203
412-381-1870
Exterior color schemes

Victorian Lighting Works
251 South Pennsylvania Avenue
P.O. Box 469
Centre Hall, PA 16828
814-364-9577

Victorian Warehouse
190 Grace Street
Auburn, CA 95603
916-823-0374
Gazebos, entry doors, stained-glass
  windows

Vintage Woodworks
513 South Adams
Fredricksburg, TX 78624
512-997-9513
Authentic designs in Victorian
  gingerbread

Warwick Architectural Refinishers
P.O. Box 35
Warwick, NY 10990
914-342-1200

Otto Wendt & Co.
417A Gentry
Spring, TX 77373
713-228-8295
Cast-aluminum street lights, benches

Bibliography

Editors of *The Old-House Journal*, compilers. *The Old-House Journal Catalog*. Brooklyn: *The Old-House Journal*, 1987.

Editors of *The Old-House Journal*, compilers. *The Old-House Journal Compendium*. Brooklyn: *The Old-House Journal*, 1983.

Brandywine Conservatory, Inc. *Protecting Historic Properties: A Guide to Research and Preservation*. Chadds Ford, Pa.: Brandywine Conservatory, Inc., 1985.

Evers, Christopher. *The Old House Doctor*. Woodstock, N.Y.: Overlook Press, 1987.

Grow, Lawrence, and Dina von Zweck. *American Victorian: A Style and Source Book*. New York: Harper & Row, 1985.

Innes, Jocasta. *Paint Magic*. New York: Pantheon Books, 1981, 1987.

Moss, Roger W. *Century of Color: Exterior Decoration for American Buildings—1820–1920*. Watkins Glen, N.Y.: The American Life Foundation, 1981.

Moss, Roger W., and Gail Caskey Winkler. *Victorian Exterior Decoration: How To Paint Your Nineteenth-Century American House Historically*. New York: Henry Holt & Co., 1987.

Ruck, Katherine Knight. *Renovating the Victorian House*. San Francisco: 101 Productions, 1982.

Vila, Bob, with Davison, Jane. *This Old House: Restoring, Rehabilitating and Renovating an Older House*. Boston: Little, Brown & Co., 1980.

Wellikoff, Alan. *American Historical Supply Catalogue*. New York: Schocken Books, 1984.

Periodicals

The Old-House Journal. Old-House Journal Corp., 69A Seventh Ave. Brooklyn, N.Y. 11217; 718-636-4514.

Victoria. The Hearst Corp., 1700 Broadway, New York, N.Y. 10019

Victorian Homes. Renovator's Supply, Inc., Millers Falls, MA 01349

Victorian Sampler. Sampler Publications, Inc., P.O. Box 546, 707 Kantz Rd., St. Charles IL 61744, 312-377-800

Authors' Biographies

Elizabeth Pomada and Michael Larsen worked in publishing in New York before moving to San Francisco, where they started the Bay Area's oldest literary agency in 1972. They created *California Publicity Outlets* (1972), now called *Metro California Media*.

Their first book on Victorians, *Painted Ladies: San Francisco's Resplendent Victorians*, was published in 1978 and is now in its fourteenth printing. The American Institute of Graphic Arts chose it as one of the best-designed books of the year.

Painted Ladies started a national trend toward beautifying Victorians. This led to the publication of *Daughters of Painted Ladies: America's Resplendent Victorians* (1987), now in its third printing, which *Publishers Weekly* selected as one of the best books of the year.

The authors present slide shows based on the books to groups around the country. A museum show of forty images from the book is traveling in the United States and Europe, and is available for bookings. For further information, please contact: Michael Larsen/Elizabeth Pomada, 1029 Jones Street, San Francisco, CA 94109; 415–673–0939.

Their next book, *The Painted Ladies Revisited: San Francisco's Resplendent Victorians Inside and Out* (Fall 1989) will celebrate the new generation of Painted Ladies that has emerged in the decade since their first book was published.

Elizabeth Pomada wrote *Places to Go with Children in Northern California* (1973), now in its seventh edition, and also writes about food, culture, and travel.

Writer's Digest Books published Michael Larsen's books: *How to Write a Book Proposal* (1985), now in its third printing; *Literary Agents: How to Get and Work with the Right One for You* (1986), now in its second printing; and his collaboration with Hal Bennett, *How to Write with a Collaborator* (1988). Michael's next opus, *The Worry Bead Book*, is being published this fall.